MMXII

THE WHITE REVIEW

EDITORS   BENJAMIN EASTHAM & JACQUES TESTARD
DESIGN, ART DIRECTION   RAY O'MEARA
EDITORIAL ASSISTANT   MARY HANNITY

POETRY EDITOR   J. S. TENNANT
ONLINE EDITOR   KISHANI WIDYARATNA
CONTRIBUTING EDITORS   JACOB BROMBERG, EMMIE FRANCIS,
                        LEE ROURKE, DIEGO TRELLES PAZ
READERS   MATTHEW COLE, MATTHEW MARLAND

COVER ART BY FRANZISKA HOLSTEIN

PRINTED BY PUSH, LONDON
PAPER BY ANTALIS MCNAUGHTON (OLIN CREAM ROUGH 100GSM, OLIN CREAM 120GSM)
BESPOKE PAPER MARBLE BY PAYHEMBURY MARBLE PAPERS
TYPESET IN JOYOUS (BLANCHE)

PUBLISHED BY THE WHITE REVIEW, AUGUST 2012
EDITION OF 1,000
ISBN No. 978-0-9568001-4-5

THE WHITE REVIEW, 1 KNIGHTSBRIDGE GREEN, LONDON SW1X 7QA
WWW.THEWHITEREVIEW.ORG

CONTENTS

STEIN

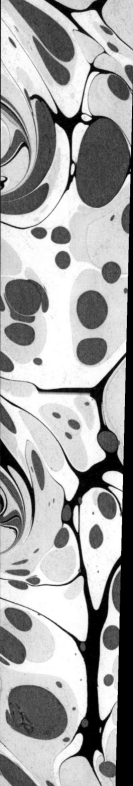

EDITORIAL

ONE of the two editors of *THE WHITE REVIEW* recently committed a faux pas by reacting with undisguised and indeed excessive envy to the revelation that events organised by another, vastly more circulated, literary magazine based in New York were the source of much intrigue and gossip. It emerged that the remark was intended not as a slur against us, but rather as an observation that literary and arts reviews are in London considered decidedly unsexy, and that it was therefore somehow admirable of us to establish one in spite of that fact. This (perhaps backhanded) tribute to our principles was fatally undermined by your aforementioned editor's response. The other editor, I should add, was a paragon of virtue in his reaction, or might possibly have been talking to someone else.

In truth, the establishment of *THE WHITE REVIEW* was not motivated by the likelihood of wild parties ensuing thereof. We wanted instead to produce something timely, useful in its belief that the sense of cultural community engendered by journals, as forums for discussion and expression, is in some difficult-to-summarise way important. The willingness of decidedly unawed people of all ages to approach us at events with questions that we can't answer, the skyscraper of submissions that sits on our office desk awaiting reading, the emails we receive defending or attacking a specific article, the continuing generosity of our supporters, the time devoted to the review by an unpaid and overworked staff – all of these testify to the fact that there is a community of people committed to the same belief in the importance of new art and writing upon which *THE WHITE REVIEW* is founded.

THE EDITORS

THE LAST WALK

BY

IVAN VLADISLAVIĆ

The writer on his last walk, a solitary Spaziergang through a winter landscape. He is going towards his favourite view, and he means to turn back once he has seen it, but he will die before he gets there. As if they know it, his last words are already on the wing, flocking around his steaming head like birds of passage. (1992)

THE SWISS WRITER ROBERT WALSER spent the last twenty years of his life in a mental institution in the town of Herisau, having been moved there against his will in 1933. On Christmas Day, 1956, after a solitary walk to settle his dinner, he collapsed on a snow-covered path and died. He was 78. The official cause of death was heart failure.

When I came across a photograph of Walser's body in Jürg Amann's book ROBERT WALSER: AUF DER SUCHE NACH EINEM VERLORENEN SOHN, it touched me even though I had read nothing of his work.

The body lies in a field of snow. The frozen block of the photograph is a dirtier white than paper and this makes it visible on the page. There is not much else besides the snow and the body: a few posts and rails, iced with snow, jut into the frame from the right; in the distance, running obliquely towards the top right-hand corner, the pencil sketch of a fence.

In the foreground, a dozen footprints lead down a slope. He walked into the photograph, into the future, and stayed there. The snow is not deep but the prints are distinct, slanted to one side, as if he turned his feet to brace himself as he descended the path, resisting gravity, feeling the world slipping away beneath his soles.

Between the last prints and the outstretched body is a clear, untrodden band of snow. He fell on his back when his heart gave in − or perhaps he lost his footing and fell *before* his heart failed − and slipped further down the slope. It might have appeared comical in the moment, this fall and slide, this slapstick coming to an end. The footprints break off in mid-sentence: his fall carried him on to the silence of a blank page. All that speaks now, eloquently beyond language, is the unfeeling body.

He lies on his back, facing away from us, his bare head pillowed in the snow and turned to the left. His right hand rests on his chest, his left arm is outflung. Beyond this hand lies his hat, fallen from his head. If he was standing up in this attitude, you would think he had just tossed his hat into the air. But he is not standing up, he is lying there supine, with his head bared and his hat tilted on its brim, and nothing expresses the fact that he is dead more coldly than the space between the two.

When I first saw the photograph, I was struck by the blank expanse of snow all around the body. Amann's text says Walser was found first by a dog, then by people from the neighbourhood, 'finally by the world'. None of them left a mark. The dog's skinny pawprints might be invisible in the snow, but did no human being rush to help the old man? Did the photographer himself set up his tripod at a cool distance

E

and take this photograph without even approaching his subject to see whether he still breathed? Perhaps the people, recognising him for who he was, stepped carefully in his footprints – it would explain why they are stamped so clearly in the snow – and gazed at him from the end of the line.

¶ I want to write a story about the last days of a writer, but I am preoccupied with hats.

The Time–Life pictorial history of the Second World War stands on a shelf beside my desk. In the volume on 'Partisans and Guerillas' is a photograph of Yugoslav men from the village of Pančevo hanged by the Nazis in retaliation for attacks on German soldiers. A notice, posted on 21 April 1941, had warned that ten Serbs would be hanged for every German soldier who died. If this measure was unsuccessful, the figure would be doubled: 'Sollte diese Maßnahme keinen Erfolg haben, wird die Zahl verdoppelt.' Maßnahme. A weighty, technical term suited to a precise levy in pounds of flesh.

It is a horrifying photograph. The bodies of seven or eight of the ten victims are visible, apparently hanged from a single branch of the same tree. Most of them have their backs turned to the photographer. Close to the foreground is a man facing us, a youngish man in a suit with a waistcoat and tie. His head is bent to one side, and the rope, which seems too thin to support his weight, rises sharply past his ear. His neck is too long: presumably the bones were dislocated by the hanging. If not for this brutally suggestive fact he would appear almost peaceful, like a businessman who has nodded off on the evening tram with his head against the window.

There are many disturbing things in the photograph. The apparent calm of the spectators, for instance. I look in vain for horror or dismay. The men in the background are soldiers whose indifference might be expected, but the old peasant woman on the right, that busybody granny out of a folktale, bothers me. She seems calmly intent, pottering beneath the gallows. Could she be the wife or mother of one of these men? Impossible. Or have I misread her expression? Perhaps I don't understand the physiognomy of fear or shock.

What pains me most when I look at this photograph, which I do repeatedly, with clichéd morbid curiosity, is that the young man with the peaceful expression is still wearing his glasses and his hat.

Of all the things that people wear, nothing is more expressive of character than a hat, perhaps because it is so close to the wearer's face, or even to his mind. This dead man's hat is small, light and jaunty, with an impish tilt in the brim. It makes the random ending of his life seem more outrageous.

The question troubles me: why is he still wearing his hat, in these circumstances, in this extremity? Perhaps I need to rephrase the question: why would a man used to wearing a hat, as most men were in those years, remove it before he was hanged?

E

He would no sooner take off his hat than his glasses. Why would anyone want to meet their death bare-headed or half-blind? Then again, he may have had no option: he was seized and his hands bound behind his back before he had a chance to think about such things. Is the hat a sign that he offered no resistance? Surely it would have been knocked off had he put up a fight. Or is it a sign of hope: any minute now they'll come to their senses and I'll go home to my dinner.

Looking at the photograph again, I am reminded that there is a second hanged man, one of those with his back turned to us, who also wears a hat. His head is jerked cruelly to one side and his hat balances on it at an odd angle. This suggests another explanation: the hat was jammed there by his murderers after they put the noose around his neck. It is meant to mock the man who has no earthly use for it, his head having been emptied of thoughts about hats, history and everything else.

¶ In THE ONGOING MOMENT, Geoff Dyer traces the meaning of the hat through American photography in the Thirties. Before the Depression took its toll, the hat was a sign of affluence, even optimism; later, the battered, buckled hat became a mark of poverty and defiant endurance. Hold on to your hat, hold on to your dignity. Dyer reproduces Dorothea Lange's photograph of two men sleeping on the cracked asphalt of Skid Row in San Francisco in 1934; one of them, lying on his side with his knees drawn up, dead to the world as the saying goes, is asleep with his hat on.

A little further on in Dyer's book, I find André Kertész's photograph of Washington Square Park in 1954. The park is covered with snow. The bare limbs of a few trees and the curved railing of a fence are inked against the white. On a slushy path, the blurred outline of a man in a dark overcoat, with his hands in his pockets.

This man looks to me like Robert Walser on his last walk in Herisau.

In a key passage on his understanding of photography, Dyer writes: 'In photography there is no meantime. There was just that moment and now there's this moment and in between there is nothing. Photography, in a way, is the negation of chronology.'

NOTEBOOK, OCT. 1992
What about the story the writer would have written on the day after he died?

As this scrap from my notebook suggests, I cannot get away from chronology.

I want to write a story about the last days, hours, minutes of a writer. But the fact is that Walser had not written anything for twenty years when he died. 'Man schweigt auch ein wenig,' Amann writes. One keeps silent a little too. A dying art. By the time he took his last walk, a field of snow lay between Walser and the dropped thread of his writing life. Clearly he is not the true subject of my story and that is why I cannot finish it.

¶ Searching the internet to see if I can establish who took the photograph of Walser dead in the snow, I find instead a photograph of the same scene taken from the opposite side, further down the slope, looking back up at the body.

The new perspective changes my sense of the place completely. It clarifies things and I am sorry to have seen it. It shows, for instance, two men in the background, wearing dark coats and hats, watching from behind a rail: even if I revert to the old view, from now on these backgrounders will be looking over my shoulder. It reveals, as well, that Walser's hat is further away from his outstretched left hand than I thought. In the other view, it appeared to be just beyond his fingertips, almost within grasp, but here the connection is broken. It also answers my question about the apparent lack of curiosity or feeling of those who found the body. There are footprints all around. I was misled by that small, indistinct image. And here is something new that I am glad to know: there is snow in the treads of Walser's boots.

On the internet, I discover that J. M. Coetzee wrote an essay about Walser for the NEW YORK REVIEW OF BOOKS. Only the Wikipedia entry on the author is more popular. And I see that the English writer Billy Childish made a series of paintings of Walser's body based on the first photograph I described to you. I move on to the Google book results. A drift of information slides out of the monitor, burying my hands on the keyboard. I think of Peter Freuchen. Google him.

E

INTERVIEW

WITH

BEN MARCUS

BEN MARCUS' LATEST NOVEL IS BASED ON A DISTURBING PREMISE: WHAT WOULD HAPPEN IF LANGUAGE, THE FORCE THAT LINKS US TOGETHER, BECAME TOXIC? *THE FLAME ALPHABET* is a story of families falling apart, and of a once familiar world rendered unrecognisable. Traumatic yet exhilarating, it invents an errant new species of fiction. Think of it as a heartrending sci-fi folktale; a myth-infused B-movie about parental estrangement. In short, it's the kind of thing only Ben Marcus could have come up with.

Marcus' books have always attracted strong reactions. His second, *NOTABLE AMERICAN WOMEN* (2002), was criticised by some for being less 'experimental' than his brilliantly alienating *THE AGE OF WIRE AND STRING* (1995). In turn *THE FLAME ALPHABET* is sometimes seen as, alongside his recent stories in *THE NEW YORKER*, a retreat into a 'realist' mode of storytelling. For his part, Marcus is doubtful about how his work has been characterised by critics. As he has put it, 'categories can have a crushing effect'. As a writer (and as a teacher of writing, on Columbia University's MFA programme) he is less preoccupied with clumsy classifications than with more immediate matters of craft. He is constantly trying new techniques, never settling for what is expected of him, never getting complacent.

I reached Ben Marcus during the last leg of his book tour, and we chose to correspond by email. I'd sit with my laptop awaiting his latest transmission, feeling not unlike the protagonist in *THE FLAME ALPHABET* hunched over his jerry-rigged radio, listening for cryptic signals that might clue him in on the plot's 'purpose'. But his art is not purposive, and there's no key that can completely decode it. He's the least dogmatic author I've ever encountered: subtle, agile, and adept at sidestepping any interpretations imposed on him. For all this, he isn't romantically disingenuous about what he does, nor falsely naïve. He emerges from our conversation as someone passionately concerned to preserve everything that writing has to offer.

———

Q. THE WHITE REVIEW — How do you begin a novel? Do you start with an idea, a 'voice', or by experimenting with a fictional space, or even a character?

A. BEN MARCUS — Despite the labels on my books, I've probably only written one novel, I think, so I don't have a great answer. There's no habit to cite. Lately I am more interested in figuring out a voice, an approach, a mode, a style, because I think that if I can lock those in place, and they feel vital enough, they will release all of the material that will make up the book. In general I am looking to escape what is too familiar, so for me form is very important.

Q. THE WHITE REVIEW — Reviewers of *THE FLAME ALPHABET* have made much of the book's 'accessibility', which supposedly sets it apart from your earlier work. But isn't there something shaky about this assertion? For me, if the new novel seemed stylistically simpler than your others, that only made it more enigmatic. Since I read it, I'm no longer sure what it means to describe a novel as being 'accessible' or otherwise. How constructive is this kind of language, and what's at work when we apply it to fiction?

A. BEN MARCUS — How constructive is it? For me, I'm not sure, but for the people who use that language, maybe it's a way to suggest that something is palatable, in the same way we say something smells nice or is sexy. It is not repellent and it is not rotten and it will not confuse you. It will behave as novels are meant to. Some of the language used to describe unusual books is laced with fear (perhaps justified) that the world's last readers will be repelled if the work's approachability is not emphasised. Let us protect and shield the world's last readers from anything that might confirm their deep suspicion that literature is roundly fucked, doomed.

Accessibility is a marketing term, but in its literal meaning – something that is easily understood – it's not very appealing. In my case, because I had not written a novel with a single narrator telling a story that moves from point A to B, it was probably easy to say that I had fled the thicket of wanking prose poseurs and was finally coming clean with a transparent narrative.

Q. THE WHITE REVIEW —— Within that narrative, some of the things we think of as 'formal' aspects of novels seem to be folded into the 'content'. For instance, if accessibility isn't a problem for your readers, it is for your characters, isn't it? Some fans of THE FLAME ALPHABET have treated its characters' communicational crises as displacements of 'writerly' or 'readerly' ones. Does that inter-pretation interest you?

A. BEN MARCUS —— The book is not about the failure of language, but its unbearable power. I'm looking at how our bodies react to something so intense; how we might not be up to handling a tool so overwhelming in its strength. I did read a review that focused on how the whole novel seems to be enacting the crisis of the experimental writer, who longs to innovate with language but is still beholden to communicating to his reader. The last thing I'm interested in is illustrating some writerly crises for the 'entertainment' of others. While such an interpretation is facile, it seems like a critical exercise more than a genuine reaction – but who am I to say? The interpretation has little interest to me, and actually there's no real crisis along those lines that I can identify with.

I identify with the problems of loyalty that arise with a father who is being sickened by his child. There are difficult human situations in the book, and that's where I tried to pour my energy. Of course any book that features language in such a weaponised form is going to court reactions such as the ones you cite – and since I've written before about difficulty and accessibility I shouldn't be surprised that people would like to read the novel this way. On the other hand, the reigning modes of narrative today would ask us to forget that language is even the medium for our books. We are supposed to not notice it – it should do its work invisibly. As much as these issues might hover around our enterprise, to me they are not eligible as overt subject matter for a novel. These are merely the local concerns of the guild.

Q. THE WHITE REVIEW —— You recently wrote that 'good literature should be a delivery system for feeling.' The phrase runs together two registers, mixing the mechanical and the organic – a combination that crops up across your work. On one level, there are living technologies like the 'listeners' in THE FLAME ALPHABET. On another, you have a way of making specialised jargon seem strangely emotive. What interests you about the interplay between technique and feeling?

A. BEN MARCUS —— I want these mechanistic, cold, strange materials to not just feel human but to be, potentially, nearly unbearable in their degree of feeling. As a writer I want to find or make feeling, and to me these objects – the contraptions and gear and equipment – end up serving as the carriers, viral agents for the feelings I'd like to lodge in a reader.

Q. THE WHITE REVIEW —— You also say that 'the creation of feeling is situational.' Has your approach to crafting situations changed over the years? If THE AGE OF WIRE AND STRING assembled multiple situations, then THE MOORS and THE FLAME ALPHABET each possess an almost suffocating situational unity. What's behind this more concentrated style?

A. BEN MARCUS —— I require myself to be mostly unknowing about this. It's not mechanistic, not something that can be broken down into a reliable strategy. If I understood it at that level of detail I'm sure it would lose all interest for me. In general I want to put things into play: ideas, situations, language, characters, which then take on volume and force. Then I follow them. But I can't really parse this any more. There's something necessarily ineffable about what makes me care absolutely about something, just as we aren't able to perfectly explain why we love someone.

Q. THE WHITE REVIEW —— THE MOORS in particular was marked by a closeness of human perspective, and its ending evoked, for me at least, a sense of heartfelt empathy. Yet some writers deride emotional sincerity as 'sentimentality'. There are also those for whom humanism represents an obstacle to innovation. How do you feel about these issues?

A. BEN MARCUS —— I can't find it in me to demonise a technique. Literary techniques seem neutral until we soil them. Execution is everything, and in the right hands I'm sure that you could take the cold, clinical approach of Alain Robbe-Grillet and make it sentimental. Somebody could write handkerchief fiction

with it. I had written my share of work that clung to the surface, resisting the interiority of the characters, and I wanted to try something different. What interested me in THE MOORS was the immense gulf between the protagonist's inner life and the world he occupied. He experiences unbearable tension from his urges and thoughts, and this puts pressure on the narrative. The close third person perspective is a tremendously interesting tool. I'd hate to think – I can't think – it's to be avoided because it can lead to sentimentality.

Q. THE WHITE REVIEW —— THE AGE OF WIRE AND STRING, which is described as a kind of 'catalogue', presents itself as a technical text as well as a work of fiction. Your work often seems to engage with scientific or scholarly frames and perspectives. What makes disciplines like linguistics, or Stith Thompson's MOTIF-INDEX OF FOLK-LITERATURE, matter to you as sources of inspiration?

A. BEN MARCUS —— Authority, certainty, expertise. It all seems so tragic to me, so vulnerable. I find a lot of sadness to be possible with these rhetorical modes. There's a desperation to knowingness, and it seems like such a highly vulnerable pose, particularly for people hurtling through the void with, if we are to be honest, essentially no real understanding of anything at all.

Q. THE WHITE REVIEW —— In 2004 you edited THE ANCHOR BOOK OF NEW AMERICAN SHORT STORIES. In terms of techniques the stories seem incredibly eclectic, but were there common criteria for selecting them?

A. BEN MARCUS —— I spent many months reading and rereading a wide range of short fiction. I canvased lots of people to try to discover the work that wasn't on my radar, both by writers I hadn't heard of and by writers I simply hadn't gotten around to reading yet. It's been a while since I put that book together, but I recall thinking that I needed to stay enamoured of the stories after several readings. I had to stay enthralled and excited.

So I kept reading, making lists. I'm sure I wouldn't put together the same collection now. It's very much a record of my enthusiasms at the time. I had grown up on some cherished anthologies, but for the most part they seemed to reinforce a single, if broad aesthetic, so I wanted to spread things out and show off the range of vital approaches – in my view – of the American short story in the last fifteen years or so. I left too many people out – some obvious geniuses. Sometimes if I felt that someone was very strongly represented elsewhere it helped me to justify their omission. At the time I didn't think my anthology had to reaffirm the choices made so well by others before me. But the whole thing is a tricky business. On the other hand I loved it be-cause it pushed me to read beyond my normal, sometimes arbitrary, boundaries and I made a lot of discoveries for myself.

Q. THE WHITE REVIEW —— In your introduction to that anthology, you posit that 'when plots are revealed they cease being plots.' Do you feel there's something essentially enigmatic in fiction, which should be protected from explication?
A. BEN MARCUS —— Yes, even though I wince at that quote, since it looks like word play to me now. I was referring to a criminal plot, a scheme. If it is revealed it is dispelled. Secrecy is paramount. It looks a bit too facile now to apply that idea to literature, and I hesitate to issue some rule only to desire to break it. That said, I do love writing that is strict with what's revealed, and I often find that kind of work more exciting and dramatic. Information can

be inert and leaden in fiction. I teach courses in which students, critiquing their peers, ask to know more about a certain character, and I frequently find that it's not so wise narratively speaking to give that information. It's not dramatic. Satisfying a reader's curiosity can be at odds with satisfying the dramatic needs of a story.

Q. THE WHITE REVIEW —— In a piece in the NEW STATESMAN, you raised some complex questions about the relationship between lit-erary 'realism' and the realities (including geopolitical realities) it's expected to represent.
A. BEN MARCUS —— I think the debate over what constitutes literary realism is, among other things, symptomatic of a larger anxiety of irrelevance on the part of writers, regardless of the kind of sentences they write. Who's the most realistic writer on the planet, dead or alive? Kafka, probably. I think the assignation of realism should only be afforded based on the effect of the work, and not its technique. Maybe realism should be an honorific.

Q. THE WHITE REVIEW —— What are your thoughts on the influence of creative writing programmes on literary production in the US? Some commentators frame this in terms of an increased homogeneity, as if such programmes produced a distinctive approach – what Mark McGurl has called 'the programme novel'. As a teacher at Columbia, do you think there's any truth in that?
A. BEN MARCUS —— Plenty of writers pursue homogeneity without the nefarious aid of a writing programme. Writers, bless us, were derivative and generic and formulaic before universities came along to stifle our originality and deprive us of potential greatness. It's wonderful to have a fantasy that without the yoghurt smoothie influence of creative writing

programmes our literature would throb with variety and originality. But, look, almost no one wants a truly original literature. Writing programme or not, different, unusual, odd, adventurous writing is usually stuffed into a puppy sack and thrown in the river. What can we legitimately blame MFA programmes for? How can we even begin to generalise about them? Is it really true that many of our young writers would be better writers if only they weren't exposed to certain ideas? Do we also ask them not to watch TV?

MFA programmes are often described, from the outside, in a way that strikes me as foreign. The uninformed view is that spineless young writers submit their work to the will of the group, who then collectively decide on its value, and tell the writer what revisions are in order. In my course, critical disagreement is expected, and encouraged. Writers learn to navigate the often drastically opposing reactions to their work. They are discouraged from writing for the approval of a teacher or group of peers. They benefit from detailed critical responses and line–by–line editing (harder and harder to come by these days), but in the end they have to decide what to do with these reactions to their work. I think it's odd to demonise the programmes so much. Art school doesn't seem to catch this kind of suspicion and derision. Do the critics of MFA programmes really care so desperately for new writing unsullied by institutional forces? How nice if that were true.

Q. THE WHITE REVIEW —— Tom McCarthy has also been teaching at Columbia of late. Can any comparisons be made between McCarthy's writing and your own? I ask because British literary influences seem less evident in your work than American ones. Do you read much British fiction? And do you relate to Tom McCarthy's desire to 'navigate the wreckage of the [modernist] project'?

A. BEN MARCUS —— I would leave those comparisons to others, but I greatly admire Tom's work. He has an uncanny ability to take provocative aesthetic ideas and enact them in narrative. There's something fierce and brainy going on, but he delivers tremendous pleasure as well, and he has classical technique. As to British fiction, I read Zadie Smith, David Mitchell, Alan Warner, Kazuo Ishiguro, and a few others, but would love to find a good list of the many, many interesting writers I'm sure I'm missing out on.

Q. THE WHITE REVIEW —— In a piece you published in MCSWEENEY'S after NOTABLE AMERICAN WOMEN came out, you worried that 'wanting to do something in writing never seems to confer the ability to do it'. Are there things right now that you feel are beyond you as a writer, but that you hope to make happen in the future?

A. BEN MARCUS —— Yes, almost everything is beyond me. I guess I'm only captivated by what I can't do. Part of what excites me about a new project is the need to learn how to do it, to try new techniques, to find a place where I feel vulnerable and unskilled and sort of stupid. I don't think I know what these things are in advance, so I apologise for that. But I am afraid of writing that seems too easy to do. If it feels easy, it bores me, and I imagine it would bore a reader.

Q. THE WHITE REVIEW —— You mentioned that you 'love writing that is strict with what's revealed'. Are there any writers in particular that have led you to believe this, that writing is better suggestive than revelatory? Who would it be fair to say are your literary influences? You're known to have an allegiance to Gaddis, but would he count as an influence?

A. BEN MARCUS —— I am not wholly aware of my influences and I don't really think about it. Gaddis, however, is definitely not one. However much I admire his work, it's in another language from mine. Part of what draws me to writing is the desire to do something I have not yet read, to work in a space that seems unpopulated, foolish as that desire might be. But the writers I return to are Kafka, Bernhard, Borges, Flannery O'Connor and Jane Bowles.

DAVID WINTERS, MAY 2012

SONNETS FROM SHAKESPEARE

BY

EMILY CRITCHLEY

I.

But thou contracted to thine own bright eyes

From brightest beams falls out desire &
to prompt our heads ripening not bumping
below bliss ∫ Clear eye & lip ∫ Drops
an angling, pools out the love contract but never
would sign ∫ About Lust ∫ Grasp it
a no-go, see him for dust ∫ The cut
the little twist the un-grasp all intricately
bound in him, around him, over.
Never a backward thought or behind.
Pulled by other things is better & out
of sight... Likes which thistle-like require
no constant ∫ change without light
winds ∫ Objects are not people
but at the start who realises ∫ Ha!

II.

When forty winters shall besiege thy brow

You don't know the finitude of love
right now but it will come ∫ Like rain
it always does ∫ Or objects lightening
in the sun's light ∫ The door below
the window next the shade ∫ Who will bar that
(vain passing airs) & be a stop
to youth? Who will pluck the mushrooms at their
height? Who will you explain that to,
take them up hillsides & down, then
trundling home & back to books - when yre
an old man going on, boring
everyone wth ravaged heart & mind?
Who will love you then if not those children
we shld have except you won't have me?

V.

Nor it nor no remembrance what it was

Unfair tyrant ∫ All those hours wasted,
as I could've told you, now come back
to waste yr peace with care ∫ For you have planned
badly - or not at all! - the change of summer
to dull Autumn ∫ So do our lives fade with
the fading of the light ∫ Yet you fritter
months & days, keep yrself apart
with work, distilling thoughts with no innate
sweetness in them ∫ & I too am reduced,
waiting on yr word, which I'll not get
till you've done ∫ O you are yr own worst
enemy! & I'm a fool to stick
burr-like to a ground whch foresight shows
is without future or memory.

X.

O! change thy thought, that I may change my mind:

Why pretend you really love anyone
at all? When you are cruel even to yr
self (tho unaware) for you take nothing
to yrself but what can lead to nothing.
No, not even after death.
Or why pretend you know how to be gracious
& kind? Is it a trick of universal
hope, read in so many others' faces,
that sure you can't leave off pretending you too
feel likewise? But it is all show.
The shade you shld offer gentle love
is taken up with selfishness & hate.
Or simply absence ∫ Just you wait ∫ Nothing
will come of nothing.

XIV.

But from thine eyes my knowledge I derive

Momentarily, stars pressure
us to tell, or not ∫ Why do we
now expand into one another,
now withdraw love or feel distance
into other kinds of difference?
Of all the strangest, what a thing desire
is - that makes us do & then not.
That stops sense right at the point
we shld be eyed with pity ∫ Your love is like
that: most inconstant of traits
beneath stars ∫ From which I predict
only a sad fate ∫ Truth & beauty
bumping like dull rocks through space,
burning everything in their wake.

A NEW IDEA OF ART: CHRISTOPH SCHLINGENSIEF AND THE OPERA VILLAGE AFRICA

BY

SARAH HEGENBART

I think the Opera Village… will lead to a new idea of art, and what will emerge will at some
point also raise interest in tourism in Burkina Faso. The school will be our centre, educating
children from Burkina Faso for whom it will open up wholly new possibilities. And who will let
us share in their works! It will be a festival for everyone all over this world when we see how
children from Burkina Faso develop their own images, learn the music of their country, build
musical instruments, start bands, record music, shoot films.
(Christoph Schlingensief, 8 February 2010)

Christoph Schlingensief was a celebrity in Germany, as famous as a pop star before his premature
death in 2010 at the age of 49. During his short life he shot films, directed theatre, staged operas,
created installations, invented performances and initiated political actions. His final and as–yet–
unfinished project, the Opera Village Africa, has been described as a *Gesamtkunstwerk*, a total
work of art, and the climax of his career. The project seeks to create an artistic centre in one of
the poorest countries in the world, an institution that will include a school, an opera house and
a clinic. The village, which includes in its mission statement the aim to 'overcome the division
between art and life', elicits questions about the status of the artwork and the role of the artist
in the twenty-first century.

Despite his domestic notoriety, Schlingensief's international reputation was slow to develop
before he was posthumously awarded the Golden Lion for work exhibited in the German
Pavilion at the Venice Biennale in 2011. Born in 1960 in Oberhausen, a small town in the
Ruhr Area, Schlingensief started making films at the age of 8. He released his first long film
TUNGUSKA — THE CRATES ARE HERE! in 1986. The plot of *TUNGUSKA*, which combines
the aesthetics of a Czech folk tale with eerie surrealism, is described as follows by Australian
Cinémathèque: 'Three researchers travel to the North Pole to torture Eskimos with their avant-
garde films.' The summary gives some idea of Schlingensief's perpetual opposition to the
norms of narrative, as well as his obtuse means of critiquing the traditional aesthetics of radical
film-making.

He followed this with another 16mm film entitled *EGOMANIA—ISLAND WITHOUT HOPE*,
starring Tilda Swinton. While the film's melodrama and misery recalls a Baltic version of
Werner Herzog's *COBRA VERDE*, its visually seductive style is evidence of Schlingensief's talent
as a pure filmmaker. In contrast to these fantastical films, Schlingensief's subsequent films
would address Germany's Nazi past – *MENU TOTAL* (1986) and 100 *YEARS OF ADOLF HITLER—
THE LAST HOUR IN THE FÜHRERBUNKER* (1989) – as well as the reunification of Germany in the
historical drama–cum–splatter film *THE GERMAN CHAINSAW MASSACRE* (1990).

Having gained a reputation for his films, Schlingensief was invited by dramaturge Matthias
Lilienthal to direct at Berlin's experimental theatre the Volksbühne. His plays included *ART
AND VEGETABLES*, *A. HIPLER*, and *ATTA ATTA*, and often incorporated film sequences into
the production. His controversial version of *HAMLET* used amateur actors – skinhead members
of German neo-Nazi organisations. The artist himself would on occasion appear on stage,
megaphone in hand, to make himself heard above the mêlée of crowds whipped into vocal
participation by the chaotic, frequently inflammatory productions.

Schlingensief soon became bored with theatre and looked to take his work into the street, leading to diverse social and political performances. Chancellor Helmut Kohl, the head of the conservative Christian Democratic Union, was among Schlingensief's favourite targets. The artist was arrested during an art performance at documenta X in which he advertised a poster bearing the motto 'Kill Helmut Kohl!' Another action targeting Kohl was staged at Austria's Lake Wolfgang when Schlingensief invited the entirety of Germany's unemployed population to join him for a swim, intending that the combined volume of the jobless bathers would cause the lake to overflow and flood Kohl's holiday home.

The Wagner family's invitation to stage PARSIFAL at Bayreuth in 2004 would change Schlingensief's life. He would later repeatedly claim that the traumatic experience was to blame for the onset of the cancer that killed him. The offer was extended by Wolfgang Wagner, a grandson of the composer and general director of the festival who took a surprising turn in his later years towards the iconoclastic: Lars von Trier and the famously unconventional Swiss director Christoph Marthaler were among those also brought in to stage productions at Bayreuth at the beginning of this century.

Schlingensief was, perhaps unsurprisingly, heavily criticised by the opera establishment for his innovative and immensely creative interpretation (he succeeded in screening film for the first time during an opera performance in Bayreuth). Yet his encounter with Wagner would exert enormous influence over his later projects. His disappointment over the conservatism of the medium's treatment seems to have contributed to the idea to found his own Opera Village.

To fully understand Schlingensief's reasons for founding Opera Village Africa, one needs to appreciate his intensely democratic approach to the arts, as well as his taste for a challenge (it's worth noting that the artist's second production of a Wagner opera – THE FLYING DUTCHMAN – took place at the opera house in the Brazilian city of Manaus immortalised by Werner Herzog's FITZCARRALDO). His work requires the participation of the spectator, who is responsible for 'activating' the artwork. Schlingensief would go to any length to encourage, even force his audience to react actively rather than passively to the piece presented to them. This participatory practice, already part of Schlingensief's performances, political actions and plays, is a key element in the development of the Animatograph.

'Animatograph' is a neologism combining the Latin term for soul, anima, with the Greek verb for writing, graphein. It might loosely be translated as 'soulwriter', and derives from the rotating stage Schlingensief developed for PARSIFAL in Bayreuth. His original idea was to realise on screen the phenomenon by which every scene from PARSIFAL's life passed before his eyes at the moment of death. A rotating stage would serve to make the flow of images possible.

The Animatograph develops the idea by presenting a number of images, around and among which the audience is compelled to walk. The key aspect is that participation is integral to the experience, which is in each case particular to the individual. The visitor is literally surrounded by the work, with the screens projecting a series of scenarios that are less part of a comprehensible story than a series of recollections or associations that the viewer must assemble and organise. Schlingensief toured the Animatograph around countries including Iceland and, in 2005, Namibia, where he constructed his rotating stage in the slums of the former German colonial town of Lüderitz and shot a never-finished film about colonial guilt and 9/11. That chaotic shoot is recorded in the film THE AFRICAN TWIN TOWERS.

¶ The Opera Village realises the Beuysian idea of a social sculpture, uniting art and life, and can be considered the culmination of Schlingensief's art in its attempt to bring all of the different strands of his practice together. Speaking in London in May 2012, his wife Aino Laberenz described why the Opera Village matters so much to her:

> The Opera Village is a place where Christoph could cross the boundaries between art and life in a very real and direct way. It is a place where there is a different credibility to life. Opera brings together very many different things: there is the handicraft, there is the music, there is the visual site of the set. Christoph wanted to bring opera back from how we perceive it in Europe, where it is placed on a pedestal, and plant it back on the ground. When he was working in cinema, he took a very distinctive approach. He was always interested in narrative structures and the question of how we can break them open. And again with the Opera Village, he linked this with illness. The Greeks perceive music as having healing power. And Christoph tried something similar with his art. That is why the Opera Village is so important to me. On the one hand, because it tells us something about Christoph; on the other, because art is such a direct language.

The construction of the complex close to Ouagadougou, the capital of Burkina Faso, began in January 2010, and follows the construction pattern of traditional African villages, according to which individual buildings are located around a protected central area. The intention is that the village develops like a snail's shell from the centre outwards. The school officially opened on 8 October 2011, marking the end of the first of three building phases which Schlingensief had planned together with Burkina Faso-born architect Francis Kéré. In order to continue the project and to begin the second building phase, Laberenz raised around €1,000,000 in the so-called 'Auktion 3000', in which works donated by artists including Matthew Barney, Monica Bonvincini, Martin Creed, Elmgreen & Dragset, Olafur Eliasson, Douglas Gordon and Patti Smith were sold to the highest bidder.

The first UK solo exhibition of a man Elfriede Jelinek describes as 'one of the greatest artists who ever lived' opened at the German Embassy in 2012, and featured a panel discussion with the director of Tate Modern Chris Dercon, the director of Museum für Moderne Kunst, Frankfurt Susanne Gaensheimer and the director of the Hayward Gallery Stephanie Rosenthal. Also on the panel was Aino Laberenz, a celebrated costume designer who assumed management of the Opera Village Africa project in the wake of her husband's passing. In our conversation, we talked about the future of the Opera Village, its status as a social sculpture, Fluxus and the total work of art.

Q. THE WHITE REVIEW — When did Christoph first raise the idea of the Opera Village?

A. AINO LABERENZ — It was a long time in development. As one can see from his art, Africa always fascinated him, but this engagement became more concrete with the beginning of his illness in 2008. We had a mutual agreement that we would go to Africa if things got too bad, but the idea of building a whole village there developed slowly.

Q. THE WHITE REVIEW — Did Christoph mean to immerse himself in existential questions, given that otherness often opens up new perspectives and creates a space for reflection?

A. AINO LABERENZ — Not necessarily. Christoph always searched for something – whether this was here or somewhere else. The concept of 'home' [heimat] always occupied him, the question of where he was coming from. Being somewhere else allows one a new perspective.

Q. THE WHITE REVIEW — Can you tell us a bit more about how the location of the Opera Village was decided? As Sibylle Dahrendorf has documented [in her film KNISTERN DER ZEIT], it was a long and difficult search to find a location in Burkina Faso.

A. AINO LABERENZ — It's true, it wasn't clear from the very beginning that we would build the village in Burkina Faso. Meeting people played a crucial role in our decision: Gaston Kaboré, a film director from Burkina Faso, was on the Berlinale jury with Christoph in 2009. This allowed us to experience the PanAfrican film festival in Ouagadougou in a new way, which was important for Christoph.

Q. THE WHITE REVIEW — In what relation does the Opera Village stand to Christoph's work in Bayreuth?

A. AINO LABERENZ — Christoph never aimed to export German opera to Africa. He talked about 'stealing from Africa' to emphasise the value we can take from it. We rarely see this because we perceive ourselves as the helpers.

Q. THE WHITE REVIEW — Do you believe that the difficulties in Bayreuth really caused Christoph's cancer? Am I right in saying that Christoph once anticipated that Bayreuth would give him cancer?

A. AINO LABERENZ — Yes, when he said what he said about Bayreuth, I had my misgivings. Working there is difficult. There is the Wagner family, which Christoph described as a very fascist set-up. They always told him that he had no idea about Wagner, and Christoph didn't really like to be told things. They wanted to tell him how to do Wagner, which caused a lot of friction. The other thing, which he thought might even have caused his cancer, is that he wanted to immerse himself in the story and the music of PARSIFAL. This stretched him, made him lose his protective shell. PARSIFAL is a music of death, and he came very close, perhaps too close, to it. Pierre Boulez supported him. But Christoph was like a sponge. He absorbed everything around him, and squeezed it out until there was nothing left.

Q. THE WHITE REVIEW — Opera has often been characterised as a *Gesamtkunstwerk* for the way that it combines different strands of art. Do you think the concept of the *Gesamtkunstwerk* is transferable to the Opera Village, given that it aims to create a space of encounter for different art forms and diverse cultures?

A. AINO LABERENZ — It is very difficult to apply the concept of *Gesamtkunstwerk* to what Christoph did. Of course, art always involves a development and things stand in relation to each other. Yet I believe that Christoph never entirely left film. He just searched for a new structure and possibilities for developing narratives.

Q. THE WHITE REVIEW — Do you think that the work on the Opera Village project tamed Christoph to some extent, given that the project made him more dependent on donations to continue the building work?

A. AINO LABERENZ — Christoph was always dependent on financial support. He was very strategic in these matters, and he was incredibly skilled at networking. Yet he would never make any arrangements that would require him to compromise his work. He did not bow to anyone.

This also applies to the Opera Village. Christoph was very impatient. At one point, the architect indicated that he didn't really care about the schedule, suggesting that we should just build as it suits us. But Christoph pointed out that the time for dreaming was over. This clarity was one of his qualities. Also, he could be quite aggressive in his endeavours. *VIA INTOLLERANZA II*, for example, is an extremely aggressive piece of work.

Q. THE WHITE REVIEW — *VIA INTOLLERANZA II* [Schlingensief's last play, in which he re-interpreted Luigi Nono's *INTOLLERANZA 1960*, an opera about racism, in an African context] has been often described as a prototype for the Opera Village.

A. AINO LABERENZ — More like an artistic exploration of particular themes. Christoph worked on this project with Burkinabés. He was very unsure about this theatre project, and wondered whether the aim to engage different cultures by staging a theatre play could be realised.

Even though one might romanticise the coming together of cultures, I am sure that there are some aspects in which we will never understand each other. I think it shows more respect to the other culture to accept and allow for this. It is important to raise differences rather than concentrate on how well we understand each other. *VIA INTOLLERANZA II* requires a readiness to be open to something new and unexpected and to stop worrying about whether a project will work out or not. It allows for the possibility of failure.

Q. THE WHITE REVIEW — Did that allow him to be flexible, to keep changing?

A. AINO LABERENZ — Christoph often asked why his view should not be allowed to change from the one day to the next. This approach allowed him to continuously explore new perspectives. On the one hand, he was pretty egotistic and determined in what he did. Even though he always worked in teams, he decided the direction. He was the author.

Some things could fascinate him like a child, while on other occasions he could act very strategically. Sometimes, he just let things happen. In his opera *MEA CULPA* he uttered the sentence, 'I hate this improvisation.' He often viewed things in the theatre as real. I remember the story of when he once saw a play by Frank Castorf, during which an actress hung from the roof. Of course, she was secured on a rope, but Christoph viewed this situation as real. He stood up and said, 'I cannot take on this responsibility as spectator. I am partly responsible if this woman falls down. I do not want to have anything to do with this.' He then left the theatre. Christoph viewed art as an arena in which something real is happening.

Q. THE WHITE REVIEW — So he believed that it is impossible to distinguish between play and reality?

A· AINO LABERENZ — Certainly! Art is real. Just think of a kiss which two actors have to exchange on stage. This kiss is real at the end of the day. And this is something Christoph took into account. He acted against established theatre conventions. He viewed theatre as something real, and treated it accordingly. This led many to not take him seriously as a theatre director. They categorised his work as improvisation or pure provocation to degrade it. Christoph never intended simply to provoke. Rather he searched for something, asked for it, realised it, and provoked by doing this.

Q· THE WHITE REVIEW — In 2002, Schlingensief performed a Voodoo ritual against the Free Democratic Party politician Jürgen Möllemann, who had been accused of anti-Semitism and was under investigation for illegal arms deals. [Möllemann died in suspicious circumstances the following year during a parachute jump.] How did he proceed there? What was his motive in staging this action? How seriously he took his performances becomes obvious if one remembers that Schlingensief's performance during documenta X ended with him in prison.
A· AINO LABERENZ — True. Christoph was imprisoned for a brief time during documenta X, where he staged a Fluxus performance under the protection of the theatre. Christoph was incredibly receptive as well as a precise observer. He was especially interested in political contexts, the framework of his time, and his environment. He was not just keen on attacking things, but deeply engaged with the situations in which he found himself. He was very influenced by the history of Germany, and its problems with neo-Nazism. Christoph understood himself as an artist with a view on these things. He considered Möllemann's behaviour to be so repellent that he responded to it in his Fluxus action.

Q· THE WHITE REVIEW — How did Christoph react to criticism? I remember an interview he gave on television shortly before he died, during which he emphasised that there was a time in which he only read negative reviews.
A· AINO LABERENZ — True. This was something one could not protect him from because he absorbed everything, and especially criticism. It drove him crazy. Looking back, I think that this has something to do with his biography. He started very early, at only 8 years old, to shoot films. It was clear that this was his medium, and he very much believed in it. He thought like a child: 'I am fascinated by something. Why are you not similarly fascinated?'

When he had to face reality, he realised that his films were not received very well. One reason might be that his films were not the typical kind of Hollywood movies, but quite experimental. Christoph looked for a different kind of narrative structure, and he encountered extreme opposition. Also, he continuously dealt with existential questions. Things were difficult for him from the very beginning. Even though he did not come from an art background, he found his own way, but his work was continuously rejected for being too non-conformist. I think that this had a strong impact on him. Also, his Catholic upbringing was a great influence – the guilt, and the requirement that you should act in a certain way. Christoph really wanted to do things right, and he always emphasised that what he was doing might not be right because it was so different.

Q· THE WHITE REVIEW — Might it be that his diversity, his ability to work in a variety of media, made it more difficult for him?
A· AINO LABERENZ — Initially, he really focused on film. Yet his art of filmmaking

contradicted the German idea of what a film ought to be like. A new transformation of aesthetics does not seem to be possible in Germany now. The times of Rainer Werner Fassbinder are long over. Experimental film was more common in the Sixties, Seventies, when it was still possible to shoot films with a limited budget. Today, making a film normally requires a big budget, meaning that young filmmakers can't experiment with new ideas. In this respect, Christoph had it much easier. He always followed his own path, and took a lot of risks in doing so. There were occasions when he hardly ate for two weeks, just to be able to shoot another movie. While the other members of the team had a fixed salary, Christoph would be the one to take responsibility, and ended up in debt.

Q. THE WHITE REVIEW — Did he have precise ideas about how his work should be handled after his death?

A. AINO LABERENZ — Regarding his films and theatre plays, he made quite clear that he does not want them to be staged again in a different way. He was adamant that his films are made for the cinema, and must not be screened from a DVD. He told me some things very clearly. Since I was part of the building of the Opera Village from the very beginning, Christoph told me that I should continue working on this project in my own way. Our relationship was characterised by profound trust, and Christoph was confident that I would continue the project. He, of course, would have worked on the Opera Village in a totally different way. I am very aware of this and I am not trying to do justice to something which I cannot achieve.

Q. THE WHITE REVIEW — What are the plans for the Opera Village?

A. AINO LABERENZ — Christoph envisaged three construction phases. There are now sixteen buildings, and fifty children aged 6 to 8 are in the first class. A further fifty will join with every new school year for the next five years. There is an art school there, which has a focus on film. I have set up a committee of advisers.

Now, I am involved with the auction with the aim of continuing with the second construction phase, focusing on building the medical centre, the extension of the school and a sports ground. Construction phase three will focus primarily on the opera house, and also a piazza – a forum for people to exhibit their own work.

Q. THE WHITE REVIEW — Was beauty something that interested Christoph?

A. AINO LABERENZ — Beauty did not concern Christoph much. He never did something in order to create something beautiful or for the sake of beauty.

Q. THE WHITE REVIEW — Yet his art is aesthetically very appealing.

A. AINO LABERENZ — Of course. He was very exact and had a very precise eye which allowed him to capture everything. But Christoph never pursued art for art's sake, or in order to make something beautiful. Such an approach can too easily result in superficiality. Christoph created art out of a certain attitude. His work had a very experimental, almost laboratory character: he aimed to use art as a means to examine things in detail. This entails, of course, an aesthetic element.

He was extremely skilled in critically examining his aesthetic view in the realm of film. I appreciated the rotting hare at Bayreuth [a large format projection that formed the climax of *PARSIFAL*], for example, as extremely beautiful. Yet, this does not really match the

ways in which one usually conceives of beauty. A lot of people obviously experienced the hare as extremely repellent [THE NEW YORKER's Alex Ross said it left him 'ready to hurl'].

Q. THE WHITE REVIEW —— Maybe the beauty of this image can be traced back to its capacity to nudge us towards important questions.

A. AINO LABERENZ —— It raises the question of how to understand beauty. Beauty is such a broad term, involving a certain degree of categorisation. Christoph granted many things an equal beauty rather than drawing hier–archical lines by describing something as more beautiful than something else. Christoph's art was independent of categories. His work with disabled people at the Volksbühne and else–where, for example, did not fit into a specific category. Yet this work possessed, for him, much more beauty than anything else.

SARAH HEGENBART, MAY 2012

NORTHERN LIGHTS

BY

NIALL MCCLELLAND

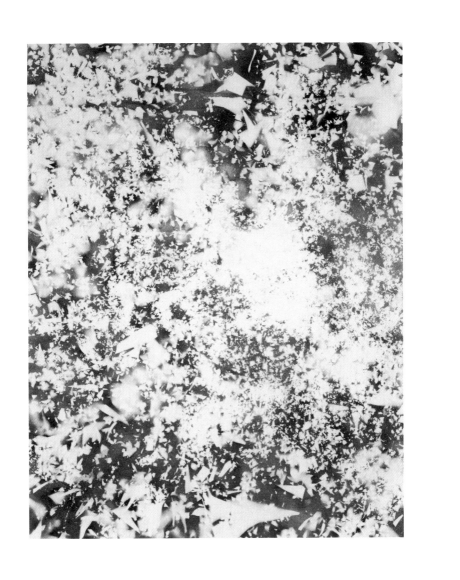

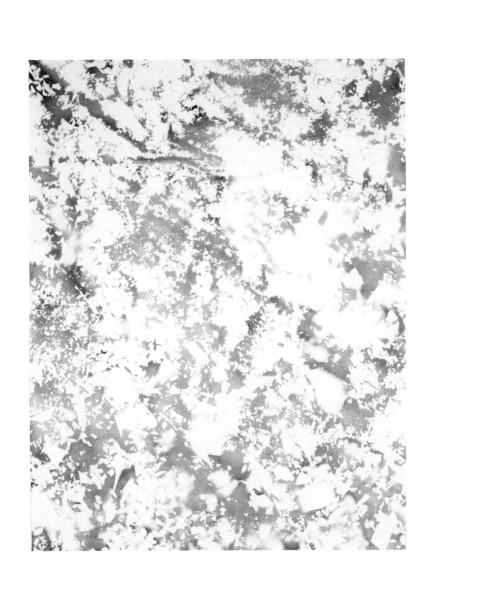

IX

TOURISTS

BY

MICHAEL AMHERST

FIRST HE TAKES A SWIM AND THEN HER, and then they swim together. The water is too cold to stay in the pool for long and yet the sun is too strong to do anything but sit in the shade. At the pool's end he presses himself against her. He pushes his tongue into her mouth and they kiss unevenly. He feels as though he's trying to reclaim something in this gesture, the heat keeping him at a point of semi-arousal. Eventually she abandons him, pushing off from the wall to swim lengths.

They've not brought everything with them, just a few presents from their parents. A few cards they maybe want to read again. Packed into her suitcase, she's brought the doves from the cake. He considers this to be sentimental, although he's brought a champagne cork, the one that his father cut with a penknife and put a fifty pence piece into. These tokens sit on the dressing table of their room.

An hour or two passes. The couple read: he a newspaper and she a tattered volume of history. Nearby a father plays with his daughter. He is white and the girl black. The girl can be no more than 7 or 8 with braided hair, while he must be over 60. For a moment they discuss whether he might be the girl's grandfather. They assume an African mother somewhere in the hotel. She will appear later, they think, as they watch the man hold the girl over the water, their concentration broken by her shrieks.

But the mother does not appear. The woman puts her book down. She takes off her sunglasses and places them by a large bottle of water. She takes a drink and her husband follows the action of her throat, the movement of her neck. She offers him some but he shakes his head. Drops of condensation fall onto his parched legs.

Last night had not gone well. Afterwards she tried to touch him but he rolled away.

'I wish you'd say something,' he said.

'It's because I love you that I don't feel the need to say anything.'

He could hear her breathing and couldn't bear the sound, a witness to his shame, his embarrassment. He considers all the things he could and should have said. Or done. But, under the revolving ceiling fan, he felt entitled to his indignation and so had nursed it in the silence.

The heat of the day is overlaid by a cool breeze that disturbs the trees and plants nearby. It picks up the dust and throws it about the streets, catches the centrefold of the man's paper and billows it between his legs like a parachute. He rearranges it, folds it, places it under a shoe in the shade. It has become hard and crisp in the sun and he imagines it combusting within his hands. He and the woman glance in the direction of the father and daughter. The father is smoking and they can hear him speaking French to the girl. His daughter's form is cloaked in his as they lie side by side on a sun lounger. He positions her next to him and takes a photo. And then another. If she tries to move he repositions her and when she gets bored and moves away he follows. She lies face down and he lies on top of her as though in a game, trapping her. She's

F

not laughing but neither does she seem distressed. He sees them watching but does not smile. There is something accusatory in his gaze and they look away.

The poolside restaurant begins to fill. Half dressed, they take a seat. They will eat steak and when offered a drink decide on gin and tonic, joking that the quinine makes it medicinal. When their drinks arrive they are syrupy and tinged with blue. In the silence, the man gets up and goes to the loo. The toilets are unisex, complete with showers, and as he stands at the urinal the little girl passes close by him. Her glance makes him uncomfortable – not embarrassed but somehow guilty, complicit even. He is very conscious of holding himself and feels this scene could be interpreted differently and in a way he has no means of guarding against.

Last night, when he'd finally fallen asleep, he'd dreamt of children. Not these children, but his own. His own unborn children dying in the heat, staked out across the burning ground, crying for water. Their lips bleeding and cracked. He'd woken feeling hot, his mouth dry. It's the same sensation he has now, as he washes his hands and returns outside.

Their food arrives and they order wine. In the heat they quickly become a little drunk. As they survey the other diners they notice a pattern. They are looking less discreetly now. The figures they stare at meet their eyes and stare back. They're not wholly welcome here. Two men sit at the bar, heavily tanned with hairy chests. They are dressed like an Eighties clothing catalogue: tight swim-shorts and overly large sunglasses. They eye the young, local girls dotted around the bar while knocking back their drinks and smoking fat cigars. There is something vulgar in their manner.

At the next table sits the Frenchman. His arms are marked by tattoos, faded against his tanned skin, like bleached writing on paper. When the girl returns he gestures for her to move, to sit opposite him. She struggles with the chair but the Frenchman does not help – he merely seems impatient. Once she is sat down he orders her a dessert, but he does not speak; she must eat in silence while he smokes.

A waitress comes over and remonstrates with him. There is an argument as she points at him, or at his hand, but he only ignores her. Maybe she is pointing at the girl. The waitress carries on and the whole restaurant turns to watch when the Frenchman finally raises his voice. When he sits up the full force of his physical presence becomes apparent. The couple think the row must be about his smoking, but there are other smokers here. The girl is no longer eating. He gesticulates wildly at the waitress, using his cigarette as a weapon. Eventually she backs off, turning to look at him as he spits into the shadow of her footsteps. When he and the girl get up to leave he threads her small hand through his and they walk around the pool and into the lobby. This is the only paternal thing he has done throughout their exchange. The couple get up from their lunch. They pretend to be bored by idleness but in truth they want to escape their isolation with one another. They speak with the

F

man on reception, ask for a taxi. They've spoken with him before, for advice on the area, places to visit. He is their friend he tells them, he loves their country. He loves Manchester United.

'Now might be the time to ask,' the husband says. But he cannot think what it is they will say.

'The man and the little girl,' they mumble together.

The receptionist squints back at them both. He doesn't understand.

'Out there by the pool.'

'Ah the man and the little girl. Yes...' he trails off. The phone is ringing.

They wait for him to continue but he does not. A conversation hangs in the air that they will not have. The woman pushes on.

'Who is she? I mean, is she his daughter—'

'Daughter. Father and daughter,' nods the receptionist. 'Father and daughter. Yes.'

The husband feels his wife has made a mistake, by giving the answer before the question. He does not need to say so. The police are mentioned. Why, the receptionist asks them, do they want to call the police? Have they had something stolen? In their embarrassment and uncertainty they are unable to say. However, the receptionist does not pursue his line of enquiry, instead telling them, 'The police must be paid. The police cause trouble. The police cause trouble for you. Why do you want to call the police?'

They look to one another. They had not expected this level of resistance. Nor does it seem inconceivable that the police will find a fault with them and not the man outside – the men gathered around the pool.

'There is no problem here,' he says. 'There is no problem.'

The receptionist raises a finger to ask for their patience. They wait a while as he speaks into the phone. At first he is apologetic, looks at them and smiles, again that raised finger suggesting it will only be a little more time. But eventually he takes his seat and jabbers into the receiver. He turns away from them, makes busy with a pad of paper. They take their leave: slow, uncomfortable. Their steps only become lighter as they pass through the automatic doors into the heat outside.

They take a taxi out towards Baie des Dunes, said to be the most beautiful beach around. It is only accessible through miles of scrubland and a deserted army barracks. Their taxi driver tells them they must have a guide, that it is dangerous. Without a guide they will need special permission from the authorities to cross the old army ground.

'Even though it is deserted?' the wife asks.

'Yes,' he says. 'All visitors must pay a permit. Without a guide it is more expensive.'

They agree to take him as their guide.

They are passing through Ramena when the taxi driver stops. It's unclear why.

They get out and walk around, amongst the chickens and children that run free on the sandy, garbage-strewn streets. People approach them with cupped hands. They tell them no. Massages are offered. Fishing trips. The fishing boats are small. Each has only one sail – large and triangular, like a child's drawing. The idea of sailing appeals to the husband but he has no voice for it. Their silence on the drive and their ready chorus of denials has made an acceptance too difficult. So they move on. The taxi driver gestures towards a cash point. It seems out of place here. We have cash, they tell him. He seems surprised. Yes, but do they not want more? Do they not wish to get more money while they're here?

They drive across sand dunes and down dirt tracks. The driver stops to point out baobab trees with their fat, gross trunks. He asks if they want a photo. Neither of them says anything, but they stop anyway and soon find themselves walking through brambles. He takes their picture and they make a play of thanking him, before they file back to the Citröen 2CV. He has to shut the husband's door from the outside and the husband nods at him in thanks.

Nothing can grow here, the man thinks to himself. And yet there is that tree that stores gallons of water for the drought and everywhere about is green with plants competing for water and light. When he woke this morning the fine hairs at his groin were glued to his stomach. They pulled uncomfortably. He pictured water spilt from an urn and crops choked by weeds. He imagined his foot landing on a snake, unseen amongst dark, shady greens. He got up and washed, turning the water so hot the shower steamed. He killed his children as he scrubbed himself new.

Eventually they pull up near some huts on the waterfront where a young man is hanging fish out on a line. He's dressed in only board shorts, his brown skin flashing white with sweat in the heat. He cannot be more than 16 but he has a man's stance. Two younger boys run about him, but the young man ignores them. Cutting the fish and then hooking them on the line. The taxi driver gives him a signal and he abandons his work and runs over. At first the man assumes he is going to try to sell them something, but he pays them no attention as he and the taxi driver speak in fast voices. The young man runs back to his hut. There are a couple of marks on his back where the skin is lighter, scarred. He returns almost immediately, looping a machete through his belt. It hangs long and flat against his shorts.

'Bandits,' the taxi driver explains and for the first time they notice a dagger at his waist, which he unsheathes and sheaths in a fidget while exchanging glances with the young man. There's no one else on the beach. There's no sign of the hotel mentioned in the guidebook. The only movement comes from a couple of people out on wind-surfs. The bay is surrounded by a crescent of rocks, which they are told keep out the great whites. The wife points her camera off into the distance: at the children playing around the fishing line, at the strip of horizon and finally at the yellow Citröen 2CV.

F

The group walk along the beach. A sandbar runs out to the rocks, on the other side of which sharks circle out in the ocean. The ocean melds with colours. The taxi driver sits on the beach while the other three walk the sandbar to the rocks. The tide is coming in and halfway along the water breaks at their feet. White foam froths at their toes. The woman and the young man are talking together in broken French. The husband nods along. They ask about sharks but the woman doesn't know the word so she makes great jaws out of her palms and the young man laughs. He's tall, the man thinks, tall and strong. The young man and the woman keep talking. She takes a photo of him leaning against the rocks and afterwards the young man asks to see it and they cup the small camera screen in their hands to block out the sun. As they scroll through the photos on screen the young man's smile widens. He is standing very close. The husband is stood at a distance from them. He's holding the bags. He follows the young man's big, dark eyes.

'We should be getting back,' the husband says. 'The water's coming in.' The sea is now halfway up their calves. He resents having to point this out, how it makes him seem and how it makes him feel. As they walk back the sea sucks great prints from beneath their feet. The man tries not to think about the great whites, the great whites and how high the tide must be before they can swim over this wall into the bay.

Back on the beach the couple rearrange their belongings, the woman keeping hold of the camera. The young man gestures with his hand. Are you ready? Will you follow now? The walk takes them through mangroves and the rusting military installation. They've already seen the graveyard for Allied servicemen: for the British, Americans and free French. Some were named, others were not. The headstones for Indian and African soldiers only give a regiment and number. Here, looking out to sea, are great walls of stone, gun emplacements and brick domes like beehives.

The husband does not like their taxi driver. The man who brought someone else in without consulting them. He speaks too quickly and is too ready to joke. His jokes are not funny and half of them come in a pidgin French that he can neither decode nor keep up with. Instead the husband is left to nod along. He is making them walk too fast. Too far and too fast. The taxi driver is wiry. What little muscle he has twitches with every movement. The young man is more toned. His calves swell with every step and his torso is lined by flexing muscles at the stomach and waist, a series of lines converging down to a shot of hair and the long, fat blade hanging from his belt.

The woman begins to complain of the heat. They've brought two bottles of water with them but both are now finished. Of the two of them she is the only one with a sun hat, which she continues to adjust. The young man watches her, ready to offer his assistance only without the words to ask. A sand snake moves across the path between their feet but they let it pass without comment. Nothing startles them now. The sun is overhead and the man can feel the blood pounding in his temples. They're out in the middle of nowhere, away from the coast, a decaying gun battery the only sign of life. Life once lived, long since dead. Earlier the woman had asked her husband to take the passports and money. This exchange happened in full view. It makes him feel uncomfortable, naked before these strangers for whom he has no language. Now he considers who would know they are here. He remembers the taxi driver stopping and encouraging them to get more cash and how the young man looked at his wife, how he smiled at the images of himself on the camera.

The young man suddenly takes the machete from his belt and hacks at some overhanging branches. The branches here are no denser than anywhere else. They have climbed over and pushed through others before. But these he cuts back. The taxi driver does nothing. His dagger is not used in the clearing; he merely bends the savaged branches until they fall to the ground. There is no expectation from either the young man or the driver for thanks or acknowledgement. They don't even look at the couple but just continue on their way. In a couple of minutes they walk up a mound and there, beyond, lies the emerald sea. Now they look to the couple, gesture with their hands. Baie des Dunes they say; the couple repeat it back and they nod. The name is passed around them all several times. Along with smiles. This is what they were bringing them to and the taxi driver and young man smile as though they had fashioned the place themselves.

The couple strip down to their underwear and run into the water. It is warm and bright but the waves are so big and numerous that the seabed is obscured even in the shallows. The woman calls out, asking again about sharks and the taxi driver waves his hands to some place far away. Yet the couple continue to swim in circles, never a great stretch out into the ocean. They glance at one another but their swimming remains a solitary activity. The man reckons he doesn't know what to do in a place like this. That his wife doesn't seem to know either.

Once out of the water, the couple stand next to each other. Their guides sit some way off. The man and woman take one another's hands for reassurance. Or confirmation, perhaps. A family plays nearby. They are European with two boys and a girl. The children fight each other and occasionally look to their parents to referee or join in. They all smile and laugh easily. The children take it in turns to charge into the water and swim far out, to where the water becomes cold and dark. The man would like to speak with them. He recognises something in them that he would like for himself. But they are too far away.

The couple and their guides travel back in the taxi. It is unclear why the young man is with them and his presence shifts the balance, the ownership of the conversation and space within the car. Halfway through their journey he leaps out. He is to meet a friend here. 'Goodbye,' he says. 'Hello. Goodbye.' He puts his head through the open window, shakes the husband's hand in both of his. The gesture is genuine and warm.

F

As they drive off the young man can be seen waving at them in the mirror. There's been no exchange of money and the thought only occurs to the man now: he should have paid him. He considers asking the driver to turn back. But it seems absurd to go back. Besides, he has an awareness that it's not really thanks he owes the young man but some kind of apology. He doesn't want to acknowledge this because it would mean acknowledging the offence.

At the hotel, the Frenchman is sat out on the veranda. The little girl is opposite him with a pastry and a pot of jam. She pushes the long spoon to the very bottom of the jar. There is red about her lips. The Frenchman watches her but she seems unaware of him. As the couple enter they catch his eye. He looks at them for a long time. They do not wish to turn away but the force of his gaze compels them. He lights a cigar. There's no sound but for the air con and the rub of skin as the Frenchman's foot plays against the girl's under the table. A sound like the brushing together of leaves or the planing of wood. The little girl spoons jam into her mouth. Her face is still and sullen. Jam tomorrow. Jam today. The couple will move on the next morning. There is no problem here.

F

COLONEL BLIMP'S
BAD CONSCIENCE

BY

MAX MCGUINNESS

IN THE DYING DAYS OF THE GREAT WAR, BRIGADIER-GENERAL CLIVE WYNNE-'SUGAR' CANDY is being driven around Northern France by his batman Murdoch, played by the Scottish actor John Laurie, remembered as the one in DAD'S ARMY who says 'Aye, but there's nae smoke without fire' (at least that's how I remember him; had I been a regular theatre-goer in the late 1920s I would have known him as a fine Shakespearean actor. His fate is comparable to that of Richard Burton, doomed to be remembered for wincing through the boondoggle of Mankiewicz's CLEOPATRA rather than for his many triumphs on stage).

'Question is whether that's the church with the double-tower or the *estaminet du pont*,' wonders Candy while peering through his binoculars at a painted backdrop of grey-brown desolation. The only structure in sight is the ruins of what is obviously a church, which gives us a hint that Candy, never exactly the shiniest buckle on the parade ground, might be going wobbly under his tin hat. This is the first time we have encountered him since 1902, when, in the opening act of Michael Powell and Emeric Pressburger's THE LIFE AND DEATH OF COLONEL BLIMP he won the Victoria Cross for exploits in the Boer War, provoked a minor diplomatic incident, fought a duel, befriended his German opponent, fell in love, lost the girl, and was handed the keys to a nineteen-bedroom mansion in Belgravia – all during one short stint of leave. Clearly, a man used to cutting that sort of a dash will have had a difficult time adjusting to the rather slower pace of trench warfare.

As it happens, Candy is now bound for another furlough but there's no suggestion of any heroic exploits this time. Sprawled uselessly beneath some kind of rain slicker in the back of a touring car, he is well on his way to Blimpdom – balding, bloated, pink-cheeked, and firmly stuck in the previous war. It would not be surprising if this little excursion, notwithstanding the waste of scarce resources, had been devised as a means of keeping him out of the way.

The character of Colonel Blimp originated in an EVENING STANDARD comic strip drawn by David Low – one of numerous young left-wingers who developed an unlikely rapport with Lord Beaverbrook during the 1930s. Following the outbreak of the Second World War Low's creation became a byword for a certain kind of reactionary incompetence, idleness, and military ineptitude (Orwell's journalism from the period is full of scathing attacks on 'the Blimp classes' epitomised by the 'half-pay colonel with his bull neck and diminutive brain'). From Left to Right, all were agreed that Blimpery must be banished in the pursuit of victory.

Having already made four successful war films, THE SPY IN BLACK, CONTRABAND, ONE OF OUR AIRCRAFT IS MISSING and 49TH PARALLEL (the latter featuring a hammy Laurence Olivier as a Québécois fur trapper), 'the Archers', as Powell and Pressburger called themselves, set out in 1942 to make a film which would illustrate the point that, in Powell's words, you 'couldn't fight new wars with old manners'.

E

Notwithstanding these patriotic intentions, the project soon attracted the hostility of Winston Churchill, not without Blimpish characteristics himself, who feared that their film would puncture the carefully cultivated image of a modern, professional 'New Army' stripped of Blimpery. The War Office thus withheld all cooperation, but both the Archers and their backer J. Arthur Rank were undeterred, even using the official attempts to thwart COLONEL BLIMP to boost publicity. 'See the banned film!' read notices outside cinemas when it was released to full houses the following year. The critics were less appreciative: 'But what is it *about*?' demanded C. A. Lejeune in the OBSERVER. More recently, COLONEL BLIMP's visual fluency and episodic narrative structure have been championed by Martin Scorsese, whose Film Foundation has funded a new print, made from the original negative, which went on release in the UK in May 2012.

In spite of his failed campaign to stop the film, Churchill did attend the premiere in June 1943. His impressions of the work are not recorded but his general reaction seems to have been one of continuing disapproval, given that he temporarily banned COLONEL BLIMP from export to the US, where it was eventually shown in heavily edited form. As Candy continues his excursion around Flanders, the next shot includes exactly the kind of detail which might have had the Prime Minister shaking his jowls. Candy's car is greeted by two fellow soldiers holding, of all things, a pair of rather fine-looking umbrellas – a pretty obvious metonym, you would think, for bungling, Blimpish eccentricity. But Powell and Pressburger are quick to confound our expectations:

> VAN ZIJL. Glad to see you, sir. I've got another umbrella for you.
> CANDY. You've a marvellous eye for loot, van Zijl.
> VAN ZIJL. Learnt from the English in the Boer War, sir.
> CANDY. Ha, where did you get 'em?
> VAN ZIJL. Off Jerries – eleven of them – brought in an hour ago. Lord knows
> where they stole them. They were using them for camouflage against aircraft.

So not only is the umbrella-wielding major not a Blimp, he is a rough-sounding Afrikaner who was presumably fighting against Candy only sixteen years beforehand. We are also invited to imagine a platoon of German soldiers taking cover from marauding Sopwith Camels beneath a set of umbrellas which they have somehow pinched from the Blimps themselves. Not for the first time, what is ostensibly a propaganda film thus veers enticingly towards the surreal, even screwball.

Arriving at his billet, Candy asks van Zijl about the prisoners. 'Uhlans, second regiment,' van Zijl replies, ordering them to be brought into the room for questioning. A cog whirrs in Candy's brain. From what van Zijl says, it seems clear that the

E

Germans, who were armed with dynamite, have managed to extract information about a nearby pontoon bridge from a captured British patrol. Candy blusters for a few moments about the indomitable courage of the British fighting man. A pause as the camera cuts to a close-up of the South African's sinister, scarred face topped off with a mop of greasy, spiv-like hair: 'The Germans know how to make them talk.'

It's pretty obvious what's coming next, but Candy is oblivious: 'Well if they are, they're cracking. It's a sure sign. Nobody starts to fight foul until he sees he can't win any other way.' For Candy, foul fighting is always something the other one does; vice and virtue remain neatly arraigned on opposite sides of No Man's Land. There is something particularly British about this kind of bad faith. Ever since the days of the Empire, claiming the moral high ground whilst neglecting to live up to its principles has been a defining national characteristic. Where else would a purportedly centre-left government suspend basic civil liberties, connive in torture, and discard the advice of its own Attorney General on the legality of invading another country just a few years after passing a Human Rights Act designed to 'bring rights home'? The figure of Blimp may be a distant memory but the same habits of what the Catholic Church calls 'mental reservation' are shared by his successors today.

Van Zijl has no need of such moral gymnastics. Aside from the dodgy foreign accent and the twisted features, another clear sign that he must be up to no good is the fact that he's wearing a raffish-looking sheepskin gilet over his uniform. How can one expect an officer with such a relaxed attitude towards military attire to be respectful of the rules governing the treatment of prisoners? Candy, by contrast, despite driving through the rain in an open-top car, looks like he's rolled straight out of a Corby trouser press. The edge of his leather holster gleams like the armour in an Old Master painting. It is hard to imagine him ever using the revolver inside.

And so begins his risible attempt at interrogation as he strives to find out what has become of his old duelling partner, friend, and romantic rival: Oberst Theo Kretschmar-Schuldorff. A glimmer of recognition passes over the face of one of the young German captives but he quickly realises that he has nothing to lose by ignoring the hapless brigadier's rambling questions. Seeing Candy's authority evaporate, van Zijl quickly signals to have him removed from the room and sent along his way like some irritating and over-talkative great-aunt. As Candy drives off to continue his aimless jaunt around Flanders, van Zijl is left to do his worst:

> Now, listen, I am in command here now and I know how to deal with you scum. I'm not a simple English gentlemen. I'm a simple South African and I can assure you that I have means to get what I want. What was the dynamite for? How many of you got away? What happened to the three men you took prisoners? Thirty seconds to reply.

E

In his oral commentary to the film, recorded jointly with Scorsese, Michael Powell notes that van Zijl's character, played by Yorkshireman Reginald Tate, had to be South African because it would have been impossible to depict a British officer in this light during war time. But a passage in Robert Graves' GOODBYE TO ALL THAT suggests that 'colonials' did indeed develop a particular reputation for brutality during the Great War:

> The troops that had the worst reputation for acts of violence against prisoners were the Canadians (and later the Australians)[...] How far this reputation for atrocities was deserved, and how far it was due to the overseas habit of bragging and leg-pulling, we could not decide. We only knew that to have committed atrocities against prisoners was, among the overseas men, and even among some British troops, a boast, not a confession.

A few scenes later Blimp and batman are stuck once again somewhere in the rear echelons. Murdoch tinkers with the banjaxed touring car whilst Candy leafs distractedly through an intelligence report forwarded by Major van Zijl: 'Four pages of confessions not worth...' The camera cuts to a close-up of the name 'Kretschmar Schuldorff', missing a hyphen and highlighted in red ink on the page in Candy's hands. Underneath, we glimpse the words 'by the British in 1916' and then, on the next line, 'to be a prisoner of war' – a neat little trick which saves Powell and Pressburger about half a minute's dialogue.

¶ The argument about the use of torture inevitably assumes a wearily repetitive form. We are asked to imagine a 'ticking time bomb' (though any half-decent bomb maker would presumably leave out the 'ticking' these days) hidden somewhere in a crowded public space. Thankfully, we've tracked down one of the terrorists who knows exactly where the bomb is and we've got him right where we want him (though a daring screenwriter would presumably make it a tough, raven-haired, almond-eyed *her*) – squirming on the other side of a two-way mirror. An expert bomb disposal unit is standing by. Under the circumstances, for the sake of the greater good, just this once, *in extremis*, all in total secrecy, never to be repeated, it is suggested that we should consider subjecting the prisoner to, at the very least, a light bit of water-boarding until he says uncle.

The situation in COLONEL BLIMP is not entirely dissimilar. Candy's benign bluster will never deliver the goods. It needs van Zijl's unspecified rough stuff to get the taciturn Uhlans to talk. And among whatever titbits about German trench design they may have coughed up, there lies a dramaturgical nugget – the fate of Oberst Theo Kretschmar-Schuldorff, who, it transpires, spends his days with other doleful officers listening to Mendelssohn concerts in a rather well-situated English POW camp.

E

In other words, there may be no ticking time bomb, but without van Zijl's brutality Blimp would never have been reunited with his old fritzy friend. For the sake of the second half of the narrative, the German prisoners must endure a bit of Transvaalian sadism. Indeed, one could even argue that it's in their interest since their confession ultimately facilitates Kretschmar-Schuldorff's transformation from haughty, embittered, Versailles-loathing Uhlan (who blanks Candy when he first seeks him out in the POW camp) to saintly, anti-Nazi exile when he returns to England in the late 1930s. If van Zijl had not brutalised them in 1918, then the film would not have its Good German to restore a bit of national honour when the Second World War rolls around. The film thus subtly solicits our complicity in the crimes of its characters. Torture works – at least as a plot device.

In a somewhat predictable twist it is Kretschmar-Schuldorff, now in residence at Candy's enormous London pad, who delivers the most persuasive justification for unleashing merciless total war on his own homeland. In June 1940, Candy prepares to deliver a radio broadcast denouncing, as Kretschmar-Schuldorff later summarises it, 'Nazi methods – foul fighting, bombing refugees, machine-gunning hospitals, lifeboats, lightships, bailed-out pilots and so on,' only to find himself axed at the last minute, simultaneously cashiered out of the army, and, in the ultimate indignity, replaced on the airwaves by champion bore J. B. Priestley. Kretschmar-Schuldorff goes on to explain that he knew Candy's broadcast would fall foul of the authorities because he had planned to say that he 'would sooner accept defeat than victory if it could only be won by those methods'. This is the moment to which the whole film has been building:

> Clive! If you let yourself be defeated by them just because you're too fair to hit back the same way they hit at you, there won't be any methods but Nazi methods! If you preach the rules of the game while they use every foul trick against you, they'll laugh at you! They'll think you're weak, decadent! I thought so myself in 1919.

Anton Walbrook, the Austrian actor who plays Kretschmar-Schuldorff, has the kind of *Mitteleuropean* mien and timbre which might prompt a certain kind of unworldly American girl to say: 'Oh my God! I just *love* the *ax*-cent!' The quavering Germanic cadences, the glorious Technicolour, and the increasingly Christ-like penumbra emanating from Walbrook's talcum-powdered head – all these elements combine to create an irresistible impression of anguished nobility which distinguishes this scene, along with Olivier's pre-Agincourt soliloquy in HENRY V and the singing of La Marseillaise in CASABLANCA, as one of the triumphs of Allied cinematic propaganda. 'Nazi methods' here find their most eloquent advocate in a character whose life has been destroyed by Hitler: 'Who', as he puts it, 'can describe hydrophobia better than one who has been bitten?' Blimp silently concedes that this is not, after all, a 'gentlemen's war'.

And yet there is something about the whole film which reeks of Captain Raynaud, who declares, when asked to justify his decision to close Rick's Café following the aforementioned patriotic outburst, that he is '*shocked*, shocked to find that gambling is going on in here', whereupon a waiter sidles up with a bundle of cash and rasps, 'Your winnings, sir.' For is it not a little rum to suppose that Candy has managed to spend over forty years in the British army without realising that 'foul fighting' has not always been the preserve of the enemy? At the very beginning of the film, he sets off to Berlin in order to confront a German double agent who has been spreading stories about British atrocities during the Boer War, namely that 'we're killing women and children in South Africa [...] starving them in concentration camps, shooting mothers, burning babies,' as the young Candy summarises it to a superior at the War Office. Notwithstanding the hyperbole, he must be aware of the notorious conditions in which Boer detainees – civilians and combatants alike – were held. This stirred considerable public outrage within Britain itself, culminating in Liberal leader Henry Campbell–Bannerman's denunciation of 'the methods of barbarism' employed against the Boers. Even the Blimp brain cannot be so 'diminutive' as to have missed all that.

In a much commented upon piece of technical bravura, Powell and Pressburger collapse the sixteen years from 1902 to 1918 into a single montage of animal heads being mounted on the walls of Candy's London mansion as he cavorts his way around the Empire. Each kill is punctuated by the crack of a rifle bullet which seems to emphasise that lions, crocodiles, and elephants could hardly have been the only native casualties of Blimp's time in Africa, just as it is rather unlikely that he really doesn't have an inkling of what van Zijl is up to in Flanders.

Far from being 'a simple English gentleman', Blimp thus appears to be an expert in cognitive dissonance. It suits him to intone blithely that 'right is might' as he leafs through a set of confessions extracted through brutal methods, just as it suited the filmmakers to portray First World War atrocities as a Boer aberration and Britain's loss of innocence as a sudden and necessary consequence of the exceptional demands of Total War. But beneath its surface of unreflective propaganda COLONEL BLIMP undercuts the hypocrisy of its own bluster. Everything suggests that Blimp, this archetypal Englishman, is a more complex and compromised figure than he lets on. Powell and Pressburger's film hints, perhaps in spite of itself, at the brutality and bad faith lurking behind the moustache and the belly.

Keeping two sets of books remains a striking feature of official attitudes towards the van Zijls of this world. On 28 October 2010 the head of MI6 Sir John Sawers gave a speech to the Society of Editors in which he said, 'Torture is illegal and abhorrent under any circumstances and we have nothing whatsoever to do with it.' He even

E

seemed to rule out yielding to the temptations offered by the 'ticking time bomb':

> If we know or believe action by us will lead to torture taking place, we are required by
> UK and international law to avoid that action and we do, even though that allows the
> terrorist activity to go ahead.

In fairness to Sawers, he had only been appointed a year earlier. He cannot be held personally responsible for the conduct of the intelligence services during the moral and legal havoc which followed 9/11 – the dodgy dossiers, the terror flights and the squalid dealings with secret policemen in some of the world's worst political slums: Uzbekistan, Pakistan, and, as is now becoming increasingly clear, Gaddafi's Libya. And yet the earlier part of the speech is filled with the kind of hedges and qualifications which betray a bad conscience:

> We can't do our job if we work only with friendly democracies. Dangerous threats
> usually come from dangerous people in dangerous places. We have to deal with the
> world as it is. [...] We also have a duty to do what we can to ensure that a partner
> service will respect human rights. That is not always straightforward. Yet if we hold
> back and don't pass on that intelligence out of concern that a suspected terrorist may be
> badly treated, innocent lives may be lost that we could have saved.

Note the slipperiness of the language here: we have a duty to do what we can. Given the derisory state of Britain's global influence, 'what we can' in this context means little or nothing.

The spirit of Blimp is still with us. Like the aptly-nicknamed 'Sugar' Candy Britain's soldiers, spies and politicians continue to insist that their hands are clean even though they know where the bodies are buried. They are happy to push a list of detailed questions under the door of the torture chamber and then make sure they are somewhere else when the hoods, electrodes and attack dogs come out. They subcontract the dirty work to the van Zijls of this world for the sake of maintaining 'plausible deniability', a sordid conceit which has been manifest in much of Britain's dealings with the United States during the so-called 'War on Terror'. The doublethink is enough to make one appreciate the rather blunter endorsements of 'enhanced interrogation' offered by Dick Cheney and Donald Rumsfeld, who memorably scrawled across a memo outlining the proposed use of 'stress positions' on detainees: 'I stand for eight to ten hours a day. Why is standing limited to four hours?' It is of course impossible to imagine such a piece of nonchalant brutality coming from a British cabinet minister. Just as well they have the Americans to do it for them.

INTERVIEW

WITH

HANS ULRICH OBRIST

HANS ULRICH OBRIST IS A COMPULSIVE NOTE-TAKER. For the duration of our interview one hand twitches a pen across a scrap of paper before him on the table, while the other frenetically twists it clockwise and anticlockwise against the horizontal. The extent of twitching and twisting increases in direct equivalence to Obrist's mounting exhilaration at the development of a scheme of thought, becoming most frenzied when patterns emerge, when one idea reveals its correspondence with another. On those not infrequent occasions that Obrist's hands are called up to add gestural emphasis to his speech I am allowed a glimpse of the leaf of paper, which over the course of our time together becomes clogged with intersecting lines, marks, scrabbles and symbols, like an elementary geometry lesson rendered by Cy Twombly.

This cryptic log of our meeting is symptomatic of the mania to record and preserve that has led Hans Ulrich Obrist, the pre-eminent curator of his generation, to record hundreds of interviews with the world's most significant artists, scientists, writers, architects, philosophers and filmmakers over the past twenty years. A casual cross-reference of THE WHITE REVIEW's all-time fantasy list of interviewees against Obrist's résumé has these names, among others, in common: Czesław Miłosz; Michel Houellebecq; Merce Cunningham; Benoît Mandelbrot; Marina Abramović; J. G. Ballard; Gerhard Richter; John Baldessari; Eric Hobsbawm; Ai Weiwei; Studs Terkel; Doris Lessing; Edouard Glissant. Which makes the prospect of interviewing him quite nerve-wracking, even before he starts taking notes.

It is, nonetheless, for his work as a curator of exhibitions that Obrist is most widely revered. He held his first show in his kitchen in 1991 at the age of 23, famously convincing Christian Boltanski and Hans-Peter Feldmann to contribute site-specific installations. In 1993 he founded the Museum Robert Walser and began work as a curator at the Musée d'Art Moderne de la Ville de Paris, since when he has organised over 250 exhibitions across the world. He became famous for his promotion of an open-ended curatorial practice that prioritises participation and flexibility. *Do it*, a project he inaugurated in 1997, perfectly exemplifies his preoccupations. Consisting of a set of artists' instructions, the touring exhibition allowed for those directives to be interpreted differently at each venue that it visited, creating a model of curation that encourages diversity and freedom. In 2006 he joined the Serpentine Gallery, London, as co-director of exhibitions and programmes with Julia Peyton-Jones, and in 2009 he was named by *ArtReview* as the most powerful person in the art world.

We met at Obrist's office near the Serpentine Gallery, in West London, at the relatively civilised hour of 9am (the curator is notorious for his Brutally Early Breakfast Club – a roving salon that commences at 6.30am). We drank more coffee than can be healthy over the course of a morning in which I was able to experience first-hand the infectiousness of Obrist's energy and enthusiasm, as well as his ability to fit more words into a minute than one would think possible.

Q· THE WHITE REVIEW — Do you remember your first encounter with art?

A· HANS ULRICH OBRIST — I started to be very interested in art when I was 10 or 11. It was during this time, up to the age of 14, 15, 16, that my visiting museums became quite compulsive. I started to buy lots of books, and I went to see Alberto Giacometti every day at the Kunsthaus in Zurich. These very thin, long figures of Giacometti were kind of a trigger to my interest in art.

Then at some point there emerged a desire, a necessity, to meet artists. When I was 16 I made a studio visit to Claude Sandoz in Lucerne and it was an incredibly exciting thing, the most exciting thing I had experienced up to then in my life. I started to ring up more artists and to make more studio visits. And it was really in '85, when I was 17, that I think I was born a second time in Zurich, in the studio of Peter Fischli and David Weiss. It was a special moment because Fischli/Weiss were making the film DER LAUF DER DINGE ['The Way Things Go'], one of the great artworks of the second part of the twentieth century. For me as a kid to come to a studio – it was just so fascinating that I thought, 'That's what I want to do with the rest of my life.' I wanted to work with artists, to be a utility for artists.

By the time I left the lycée it was all clear; I knew I wanted to become a curator. I had met Alighiero Boetti when I was 18 and that was another sort of epiphany, as was meeting Gerhard Richter that same year. Richard Wentworth was a huge inspiration to me, as to so many artists.

Q· THE WHITE REVIEW — But you continued on to university, where you studied Sociology and Politics. Was it a deliberate decision to read something at least superficially unrelated to the arts?

A· HANS ULRICH OBRIST — I didn't really know where to start as a curator, because I had this feeling that everything had been done. I had always been fascinated by Hans Binswanger, a professor at the University of St Gallen, and his pioneering work on sustainability and the limits of growth, and I wanted to study a subject I would never do autodidactically, as I would do with art. I never had the courage to just read books on economy and the social sciences, and I wanted to understand the world.

Q· THE WHITE REVIEW — Have you always felt compelled to try and make sense of the world?

A· HANS ULRICH OBRIST — In some way I think it dates back to an experience I had as an 8-year-old kid, when I first visited the famous Abbey Library at Saint Gall, in Switzerland. You had to put on these felt shoes to enter the library – almost like a Joseph Beuys installation – and they would give you white gloves to look at the medieval books. I was fascinated by the idea that these monks wanted to know everything. It was at least theoretically possible in the Middle Ages to know everything that was known, whereas now we live in a very specialised society, with an abundance of information, in which none of us could know everything.

Q· THE WHITE REVIEW — You talk about yourself as an autodidact, at least in relation to art, but there's this compulsion as well to broaden out the sphere of what art constitutes. I wonder if the Interview Project is a means of continuing that education, allowing you to learn from people in different disciplines. How does that relate to your attitude as a curator and, more generally, your engagement with the art world?

A· HANS ULRICH OBRIST — When I started I

would always talk to artists, and talk to artists, and my life became this infinite conversation. Whenever I had time I would go to studios, go to openings, and have these infinite conversations... All my exhibitions grew out of these conversations, starting with KITCHEN SHOW, in 1991, and including things like the Monastery Library exhibition [of Christian Boltanski in the library at Saint Gall], my show with Gerhard Richter in the Nietzsche House, the exhibition on an airplane with Boetti and an exhibition in room 763 at Hotel Carlton Palace when I arrived in Paris in 1993. I invited everyone to my hotel room and showed them around. Strange exhibitions in unusual locations. All of these things came out of conversations with artists.

I realised that all these conversations were being lost, because I only took notes. When Boetti died, it was a watershed moment. I realised we had had so many conversations, and I had lost a lot of that. My memory is not perfect. Recording conversations became a protest against forgetting. I wanted to keep traces.

Q. THE WHITE REVIEW — There seems to be an interesting relationship between the idea of archive and what that achieves. I wonder how you use these archives in your practice now, how you return to them?

A. HANS ULRICH OBRIST — There has always been a sense of urgency in my activity, a conviction that every day could be the last. I've always believed, as a curator as in any activity, that when you start to look back it prevents you from moving forward. So I've always frantically produced archives and yet not really looked backed on them. I've not actually watched much of those 2,000 hours of film, but I know they are there. And it's interesting that my whole attitude as a curator

is active: there is a strong desire to do certain exhibitions and a strong desire to do certain interviews. It's important to say that very few of these interviews are commissioned for someone else; I just do them because I need to do them, and out of curiosity.

Q. THE WHITE REVIEW — How did the book series come into being?

A. HANS ULRICH OBRIST — Walther Koenig [who publishes the Conversation series] is interested in the fact that I talk to the same artist again and again. That led to the Conversation series, where several of my interviews with one artist are put together in a single book.

That's the answer to your earlier question, in fact: that was the first time I looked back. I've got twenty-two Dictaphone machines. I have them everywhere. I have them at home, one in each suitcase, one at my parents' house... I never leave the house without one. I have about fifteen digital cameras and hundreds of memory chips and hard drives. It is chaotic. And then with the interview books we started to look back, and that was suddenly a very interesting experience, activating that archive.

Q. THE WHITE REVIEW — You touched earlier upon the limits of knowledge, and you mention now the role of the editor in compiling material in a useful fashion. It seems like a particularly pertinent point given that we live in the digital age, with this vast store of knowledge easily available to us all. But that raises the question of how this superabundance of knowledge is to be channelled, and who, if anyone, is responsible for that. Is that the role of the curator? Is this among the reasons that the curator has come to prominence, because people are increasingly overwhelmed by information and need a mediator?

A. HANS ULRICH OBRIST — The notion of the

curator has changed a lot. When I told my parents I was going to be a curator, they thought I wanted to enter the medical profession. The fact that the profession was quite obscure at the time led to *A Brief History of Curating* [in which Obrist collected together interviews with influential curators], an attempt to uncover the history of curating. But the use of the term 'curator' has grown exponentially over the past couple of years. It has to do with navigation; we live in an age with an abundance of information and people need guides, editors.

The big question now is how are we going to edit for the digital world? Because there will be a different way of editing, of selecting. With these extraordinary abundances of information how can one make sense of my 2,000 hours of film, without just adding more noise? What could we do with the tapes I made with Cedric Price? I would always go at 8am to his office, the famous all-white room, and we'd have a whiskey and record the interview. Sometimes he would make a demonstration with umbrellas, or he'd show me his boxes full of drawings, it was really magical. He never wanted to do more than half an hour, so we did twenty sessions of thirty minutes.

I have ten hours of tape now, but to just throw them online would be pointless. One possible way around it is by tagging phrases and themes, so that the viewer can skip to them. Together with the University of Karlsruhe and the Institute of the Twenty-first Century we started to tag all the material, so now you can type in 'Fun Palace' and get the five passages in which he talks about that, or 'Umbrella' and see the one moment that Cedric opens his umbrella on a sunny day in his office.

That gives me a lot of hope that I can crack the issue of what to do digitally with these interviews in the long run. If you could tag all 2,000 hours properly then you create a situation where the living talk to the dead.

Q. THE WHITE REVIEW — This idea of tagging is interesting because it automatises the method of selection, and in fact removes the curator from the process. To borrow a phrase from Walter Hopps, it frames abundance rather than annihilates it. The viewer is allowed to navigate his or her own course without having it dictated to them. I wonder how that relates to your own practice, this idea of removing yourself from the process of curating?

A. HANS ULRICH OBRIST — It is a huge topic, the notion of self-organisation, and the idea of framing abundances is very beautiful. It has to do with the question of how it is possible eventually, as a curator, to escape the idea that you are a master planner. Historically, the curator was the one who made the checklist, who created the master plan. That notion of self-organisation was actually realised in architecture in the 1950s and 1960s. Cedric Price called it the 'Non-Plan' [in his book of the same name, published 1968]. That was a great inspiration for me.

I've tried to bring these urbanists' experience of self-organisation into curating. I made a transfer. At some point I realised, through Alexander Dorner, that if you want to understand the forces that are in effect in art, it is important that you go into other disciplines. And that's when I started to extend my interview approach into science, into literature, into music.

With regards to exhibitions, I have tried to create 'temporary autonomous zones', as we did with *Cities on the Move*, in which there is space for change and movement that is not premeditated. It has to do with energy: very often when you have an exhibition with a master plan, that master plan is finished five months before the opening. The exhibition opens and it feels dead. I'm obsessed by energy and I always want my exhibitions to have energy and be about energy. With CITIES ON THE MOVE, or even with more recent shows like the Lyon Biennale, you bring in new models for different rules of the game. It's more dynamic then because there are feedback loops, as Cedric would say [Price drew on early cybernetics to theorise a style of architecture that would be flexible, reactive and responsive to the needs of its inhabitants].

Q. THE WHITE REVIEW —— Price promoted dynamic over static systems, which seems to tie in with Alexander Dorner's maxim that the role of the museum is to build bridges between the arts and other disciplines. It's noticeable how many of the curators you interviewed in A BRIEF HISTORY OF CURATING started out in different disciplines and found themselves organising exhibitions almost by accident. That to me seems tremendously important, the fact that people like Lucy Lippard could bring entirely different energies and experiences to the practice. Do you think that, as curation has become this subject to be studied academically, some of that energy is being lost? Whether the influence of different disciplines is being compromised by curation being profession-alised, by its being a career option subject to set texts and established principles?

A. HANS ULRICH OBRIST —— That is a risk but at the same time I'm optimistic, because there are so many possibilities. There will be, and there are, curators who find completely new avenues. Look at the internet, for example: there is so much potential there for inventing new shows. The only thing which would worry me is if curating became too disconnected from art. Curating is not an autonomous discipline; it is a profoundly hybrid discipline. It is, by

necessity, defined by its relationship to artists. Without art there is no curating, and without dialogue there is no curating.

Q. THE WHITE REVIEW —— You've said previously that 'memory is very radical right now' – could you expand upon that?

A. HANS ULRICH OBRIST —— I suppose it has to do with something Rem Koolhaas once said. He thinks information doesn't necessarily produce memory, that maybe amnesia is widespread in the digital age. It also arose from a conversation I had with Rosemarie Trockel, who said that I should go and interview really old people, those who have seen the most. Since that conversation I've visited thirty-eight people who are either centenarians or in their mid-to-late nineties, including Albert Hoffman [the inventor of LSD] and Nathalie Sarraute, someone who has been too widely forgotten. The more of these interviews I did, the more I realised that these people don't have so much presence online, which is equivalent now to a kind of collective amnesia. The interview project, like curating, is a way of working on memory, a protest against forgetting.

Q. THE WHITE REVIEW —— There's a Calvino quote, 'a world without forgetting is hell'. We're particularly conscious now of this constant push and pull between the necessity to forget things, to move on, and the importance of memory if we're to achieve any kind of progress. You talked before about the creative block that can come with the awareness of so many things having been achieved, and the feeling that there is nothing new left to do: is that problem likely to become more prevalent with the availability of information, of documentation now?

A. HANS ULRICH OBRIST —— I've observed that my activity is often about oxymorons.

This whole conversation has had a lot to do with oxymorons. We've talked about self-organisation: to talk about curation and self-organisation is itself an oxymoron, because curating is about selecting, about deciding. I think, to use another oxymoron, that you have to remember things before you are able to forget them.

Curating is full of these tensions, like broad depth, or deep breadth. I've worked with Gerhard Richter for twenty-five years, but I also try always to open up to new generations. In this sense my practice is both a continuation of one relationship, and an open system.

Q. THE WHITE REVIEW — There is this recurring idea of the curatorial process being the creation of a framework within which things can happen freely. If we can return to another oxymoron: we live in an increasingly globalised world, but globalisation has this tendency toward homogenisation. Your work, both as a curator and interviewer, has this enormous scope, reaching across generations and cultures: how do you use that form to encourage difference and variety rather then discourage it?

A. HANS ULRICH OBRIST — Edouard Glissant's work gives me the courage to believe that one can actually enter into a global dialogue without erasing difference. These forces of globalisation are very much in effect in the world of exhibitions. The way that shows tour is evidence of that – our Serpentine exhibition, INDIAN HIGHWAY, which I co-curated with Julia Peyton-Jones and Gunnar Kvaran, has now been through six cities and is on its way to a seventh, in China. The important thing is that the show is defined not as a created, boxed exhibition which goes from A to B to C to D without changing, which would be an expression of that homogenising globalisation, but instead that wherever it goes it enters into a dialogue with the local community. In each case the show changes: there is each time a new artist who organises another artist-run exhibition. We've defined the rules of the game, but not the outcome. Perec is always with me!

Q. THE WHITE REVIEW — Was CITIES ON THE MOVE the beginning of that?
A. HANS ULRICH OBRIST — The beginning was really LIVE/LIFE [a 1996 review of Britain's artist-run spaces at Musée d'Art Moderne de la Ville de Paris]. Each time the show had a new incarnation, a show within the show. It was very organic, there was never a checklist, not even the day of the opening, no one had a checklist, it drove people completely nervous. So LIVE/LIFE was the beginning and led to CITIES ON THE MOVE. Somehow it never stopped and keeps changing.

The same really applies to the Interview Project, this notion of rules changing, different formats. I'm driven by the idea of inventing new formats. We can change the format of an interview by making the interview very long, or by changing the location so that it is in a very unexpected location.

I've done interviews on airplanes: I was with Pierre Huyghe on a flight to New York from Paris and the rule was that we would not be allowed to sleep from the moment the plane took off until it landed. I asked the stewards and stewardesses to put some questions to Pierre. And so the flight duration determined the interview.

There are many different possibilities, from the running interview, to the swimming interview, to the rowboat interview, to the taxi interview, to the airplane interview, to the many coffee house interviews. Changing the format resists homogenisation.

Q. THE WHITE REVIEW — And the Interview Marathon is part of that?

A. HANS ULRICH OBRIST — We've had Interview Marathons in Delhi, in Dubai, in Sardinia, in Germany, some on my own, some with Rem Koolhaas. I realised at the Serpentine in London that the Marathon could go far beyond the idea of an interview, and that the Marathon can actually become a group show. I became very interested in this idea that group shows can be related to time. The Marathon in London became an ever-changing group show, involving artists, writers, philosophers... And the artists are given a set time, and each year there is a different topic, from poetry to maps, and this year it is memory. Memory is often associated with the past, we think of it as static, while actually it is a super-dynamic process.

Q. THE WHITE REVIEW — This idea that memory is dynamically generated out of the present is beautiful. I was interested by this idea of the Marathon Project as an exhibition, as a group show; I wonder if you conceive of the Interview Project more generally as an exhibition? If it qualifies as an exhibition or if you think it could ever be conceived as an exhibition?

A. HANS ULRICH OBRIST — In my mind there's a department of interviews and a department of exhibitions, and in the interview department there are lots of sub-departments and the key distinction I would say is between public and private interviews. Most of my interviews or conversations happen without an audience. The audience enters into it much later, if and when we publish it. But the conversations are very private, a sense of intimacy is important. No matter how these interviews come to be, they all enter into the archive and can then create other sorts of connections and can one day, hopefully, through the tagging become useful to others.

I was always really interested by John Dos Passos's USA TRILOGY – this very sort of polyphonic novel, newsreel mixed with fiction. I've always hoped this tagging thing could work, that my entire Interview Project could become not so much an exhibition, but this one polyphonic novel.

Q. THE WHITE REVIEW — That seems again to be about disrupting or cutting up time. You've mentioned elsewhere that conversations allow you to liberate time. Is that not related to this idea of polyphony, history and difference?

A. HANS ULRICH OBRIST — Homogenising forces are effected not only in terms of space but also in terms of time. In the Nineties, the beginning of my activity was about resisting the homogenisation of space by doing exhibitions in places where they are least expected. Then I realised that maybe curating could also address the homogenisation of time; in conversation with artists I realised that more and more artists were interested in exhibitions dealing with time and not space. Out of these conversations grew the Marathons, but also my collaboration with the Manchester International Festival. It's no coincidence that in the Nineties I organised all these Biennales, while in the 2000s my group shows shifted into a festival context. In ELEVEN ROOMS [2011] Klaus Biesenbach and I invited artists to Manchester and gave them each a room. In each of these rooms behind the door there was a living sculpture.

That was the next step after IL TEMPO DEL POSTINO [co-curated with Philippe Parreno] at which we gave each artist approximately fifteen minutes. Matthew Barney took an *every day*

20 page

Hans-Ulrich Obrist Interview

TWR. You didn't have a traditional training in the visual arts, so how did you initially come to be involved in the art world?

HUO. I started to be very interested in art was when I was ten or eleven. It was during this time, up to the age of fourteen, fifteen, sixteen, that my visiting museums became quite compulsive. I started to buy lots of books, and I went to see Giacometti ~~again and again~~ at the Kunsthaus in Zurich. These very thin, long figures of Giacometti were kind of a trigger to my interest in art.

Then at some point there emerged a desire, a necessity, to meet / artists. When I was sixteen ~~or seventeen~~ I made a studio visit to a Swiss artist in Lucerne and it was an incredibly exciting thing, the most exciting thing I had experienced up to then in my life. I started to ring up more artists and to make more studio visits. And it was really in '85, when I was seventeen, that I think I was born a second time in Zurich, in the studio of [Peter] Fischli & [David] Weiss. It was a special moment because Fischli/Weiss were doing the film **Der Lauf der Dinge** ['The Way Things Go'], one of the great artworks of the second part of the twentieth century. For me as a kid to come to a studio... It was just so fascinating that I thought, 'that's what I want to do with the rest of my life'. I wanted to work with artists ~~and be useful~~, to be a utility for artists.

By the time I left the Lycée it was all clear, I knew I wanted to become a curator. I had met Alighiero Boetti when I was eighteen and that was another sort of epiphany, as was meeting Gerhard Richter. Richard Wentworth was a huge inspiration to me as to so many artists. My ~~being so young opened a lot of doors, because~~ it ~~seemed so ridiculous [to the artists], this teenager obsessed with art.~~

TWR. But you continued on to university, where you studied Sociology and Politics? Was it a deliberate decision to read something at least superficially unrelated to the arts?

HUO. I didn't really know where to start as a curator, because I had this feeling that everything had been done. So ~~I thought that if I was to be very clear about it, and also to calm my parents, I should go to university.~~ At the same time I also wanted to study a subject I would never do autodidactically, as I would do with art. Because I never had the courage to just read books on economy and on social science, and I wanted to understand the world.

The same year

Claude Sandoz

BINSWANGER

I was fascinated by Professor Binswang

his pioneering work on sustainability & limit of Growth

1a / | BEST REGARDS Hw

hour and some artists did very short pieces, only a minute or two long. It's not that I 'left' space, it is just that time presents an additional dimension, and one in which homogenising forces are also at work. I believe exhibitions can help to liberate time from these forces.

It all goes back to Alexander Dorner, when he says we need to bring all these different feeds together. That's difficult today: if you do a conference by an architect, the architecture world comes. How can you make sure that that doesn't happen? With the Marathons we very often have people from the literature world, the music world, the art world: they all come together. Dorner is among the figures I always return to, another being Félix Fénéon.

Q. THE WHITE REVIEW — The editor of *LA REVUE BLANCHE*...

A. HANS ULRICH OBRIST — What is also so interesting about Fénéon is that he's a model for the twenty–first century curator. He was a curator of literature, he was a curator of art, he connected these things to science. He also understood that the curator is in a very strange negotiation between invisibility and visibility, that the curator is the catalyst and that the catalyst at some point disappears. He assumed so many different roles: he was an exhibition organiser, he was a poet, a writer, he was a close friend to the artists. Out of his friendships he developed *LA REVUE BLANCHE* and created books and exhibitions, all these different dimensions.

John Rewald, the great biographer of Cézanne, did the same thing I wanted to do. He protested against the forgetting of Félix Fénéon. Fénéon was somewhat forgotten be–fore Rewald came to Paris in the 1970s and looked him up in a telephone book and went to see him. Fénéon didn't really want to appear any more but Rewald had these conversations

with him anyhow and then wrote this great book [*FÉLIX FÉNÉON, L'HOMME QUI DÉSIRAIT ÊTRE OUBLIÉ*]. That's what we can do, through curating or interviews or by other means I haven't even thought of: we can act against the forgetting of people like Cedric Price. There is always the question, as a curator, of how one can be a utility. John Rewald was a great utility to Félix Fénéon, yet at the same time Fénéon was an incredible inspiration to him.

Q. THE WHITE REVIEW — My final act, in this interview of the interviewer, is to ask you the question that you always ask your interview subjects: what is your unrealised project, the thing that you've always wanted to do but have been unable to complete thus far?

A. HANS ULRICH OBRIST — I have to give two answers: one as a curator, one as an interviewer. There are many unrealised interviews, though perhaps the biggest is Jean–Luc Godard. It has just never happened, but I am hopeful. A Godard interview is difficult but it is not *completely* impossible [Godard is notoriously averse to interviews] but then there are the impossible interviews, like On Kawara. In fact the cover of the first volume of interviews is a secret homage to On Kawara: there is a picture of a microphone, with the word ON.

Had you asked me the same question two years ago I would have answered Hans–Peter Feldmann. He and I have been friends and in close dialogue for over twenty years. I met him just after my *KITCHEN SHOW* with Christian Boltanski and Richard Wentworth, but he has always refused to do an interview. Then suddenly two years ago he said, 'I've found the solution: you ask me the question and I answer with the image.' So I asked him one hundred questions and he answered me in images and that became a book. My last interview with Louise Bourgeois was just me asking her questions and her sending me a drawing by email. So there is a whole series of post-symbolic interviews that I want to explore: that is an unrealised project.

So many different types of exhibitions unrealised, either too big or too small, or censored – self-censored projects, the things I didn't dare to do. I've always had the dream to do a big exhibition: there was the Crystal Palace in 1851, Cedric Price's Fun Palace in 1961, and I want to create a third palace, the Palace of Unbuilt Roads. It will be a palace built to be filled with thousands of unrealised projects. We've actually been quite close to realising this project, but each time I get close it falls through. It remains unrealised, it is the meta-unrealised project.

BENJAMIN EASTHAM, APRIL 2012

THREE POEMS

BY

GIOCONDA BELLI

(*tr*. J.S. TENNANT)

CALMA

Calma.
Permití que tus manos
encuentren sus reptiles ancestros
para que se deslicen
como serpientes
por la profunda espesura de mi pelo.

La cúpula de mi templo
es el ámbito que encierra
la sacrosanta arca de la alianza.
Mis orejas, los minaretes
para los cánticos más húmedos
de tu lengua.

Invertí el órden.
de arriba abajo
hacé tu camino de ladrón
descendiendo desde la bóveda
colgado de la más larga de mis pestañas.

En el tobogán del cuello
deslizate como el sabio que busca inutilmente
la cuadratura del círculo
y lanzado fuera de vos mismo
recorré el valle tenso
que yace entre mis dos pechos.

En el cenote de mi ombligo
depositá un beso mercurial
que se enrede por los laberintos hondos
por los que se llega a la misma memoria
del vientre de la madre.

CALM DOWN

Calm down.
Let your hands
rediscover their reptile forebears
to slither
like snakes
across the heavy depths of my skin.

The dome of my temple
is the circumference enclosing
the sacrosanct ark of the covenant.
My ears: minarets
for the dampest canticles
of your tongue.

Reverse the order.
From top to toe
lower yourself
like a thief
suspended from my longest eyelashes.

Slide on the toboggan of my neck
like the seeker who vainly attempts
to square the circle
and, thrown out from yourself,
traverse the taut valley
that lies between my breasts.

In the well–spring of my belly–button
place a mercurial kiss
that can wind its way into the deep labyrinths
leading to the memory
of my mother's womb.

De allí en adelante
dejate guiar por la locura
por la avaricia de tu paladar
por tu vocación de explorador
en busca del Centro de la Tierra.

Sé el minero que a tientas
descubre las vetas de sal
que el mar olvidó en las cuevas femeninas
donde la vida tiene su refugio.
Aferrate a la húmeda rosa de los vientos
más poderosa que los huracanes del Caribe
o los maremotos del Pacífico.

Calmá tu sed y tus furias en mí,
en el fondo de musgo y algas
que gimiendo te devuelve
a la breve, eterna seguridad
del paraíso perdido.

From there on in
let yourself be guided by craving
by the greed of your mouth
by your explorer's vocation
in search of the Centre of the Earth.

Be the miner who – gropingly –
discovers the seam of salt
left behind by the sea in the feminine caves
where life takes refuge.
Cling to the wet rose of the winds:
more powerful even than Caribbean hurricanes
or tidal waves in the Pacific.

Sate your thirst and rage in me,
in the depth of moss and algae
which – moaning – returns you
to the brief, eternal safety
of that lost paradise.

LOS GUIJARROS DEL DIA

Soy una solamente.
No puedo más que estar aquí.
Si fuera muchas podría hacer tantas cosas:
–manifestarme en Teherán
–protestar en Irak
–ser judía y exigir el estado Palestino
–ser Palestina y exigir el fin de los agravios
–ser Afgana, rasgarme la burka y arriesgarme a la lapidación
–ser norteamericana y exigir el control del lucro y la ambición

Pero soy una.
Sólo soy dueña de la patente de corso de mi patria minúscula
hacia allá encamino mis palabras como guijarros
mi amor grande e insuficiente para sus necesidades
mi ojos que salidos de sus órbitas viajan a recoger
paisajes que yo enjuago delicadamente
que alojo en la más luminosa zona de mi retina.
Tantos años llevo acumulando este país, comiéndomelo, rumiándolo,
llorándolo, abrazándolo, arrullándolo.
Tantos años y siempre se me escapa,
rebelde, joven, díscolo
perseguidor de ilusiones que jamás se realizan.
Lo sigo por los mercados,
lo veo desarrapado, desalmado y sucio
pide y golpea después con el garrote al que se saca las monedas de la bolsa,
Se para en las esquinas a decir los poemas más hermosos
y en la noche escupe veneno y mentiras, limpio y pulcro, tras los
micrófonos.

P

PEBBLES OF DAY

I'm just one person.

I can't be everywhere.

If I were many I could do so many things:

– demonstrate in Tehran

– protest in Iraq

– be Jewish and demand the Palestinian State

– be Palestinian and demand an end to the injustices

– be Afghan, rip up my burka and risk being stoned

– be North American and demand control of profit and ambition

But I'm one person.

I've only been granted special rights in my diminutive homeland;

it's there that I direct my words like pebbles

my great and insufficient love for his needs

my eyes that, given total licence, roam to take in

landscapes I delicately cleanse

that I house in the brightest part of my retina.

I've been accumulating this country so many years, eating it, ruminating it,

crying it, hugging it, whispering sweet nothings to it

so many years, yet always it escapes me:

rebellious, young, unruly

pursuer of dreams that never come to pass.

I follow him through markets;

I see him in rags, dirty and heartless

he begs, and then bites the hand that offers;

he stops on street corners to recite the most beautiful poems

and by night he spits venom and lies, crisp and clear, behind

microphones.

Bellas y desoladoras son las visiones
de este mapa de cristales cortantes.
Su azúcar me corroe la sangre.

Quisiera estar en tantas partes.
Pero soy una solamente.
Y sólo tengo un saco de guijarros que cada día afilo,
pulo con mi aliento cargado de visiones
y desperdigo al viento.

Visions of this map of jagged glass
are beautiful and heart–rending.
Its sugar corrodes my blood.

I'd like to be in so many places.
But I'm just one person.
And I've only got a bag of pebbles I smooth daily,
that I shine with a breath heavy with hopes
and scatter to the winds.

APOCALIPSIS

Hace unas horas
el Apocalipsis
el llanto y crujir de dientes de nuestro amor
en el día del Juicio Final.

La conversación. El vino. La rabia
las explicaciones. La palabra y el corazón
tratando de encontrar un idioma común.
El alegato de inocencia:
vos entrando al estrado
con tu defensa simple y llanamente estructurada
y yo perdonándote una vez más
pensando que me he equivocado
que te he juzgado muy duramente
depositando la túnica
con que pensé mandarte a la horca
suavemente sobre la silla
junto con la ropa
que me quito
para entregarme a tu amor
una vez más.

THE APOCALYPSE

Just a few hours ago
the Apocalypse
the wailing and gnashing teeth of our love
on Judgement Day.

Conversation. Wine. The mania
of explanations. Speech trying to find
a common language with the heart.
The assertion of innocence:
you taking to the stand
with your straightforward and well-structured defence
and me forgiving you once again
thinking I'd got it wrong
that I'd judged you too harshly
draping my gown
(I'd planned on wearing it to condemn you to the gallows)
gently over the chair
next to the clothes
I take off
to surrender myself once again
to your love.

XII

Ursonate

einleitung:

Fümms bö wö tää zää Uu,

        pögiff,

            kwii Ee.

Oooooooooooooooooooooooooooooooo,   6

dll rrrrrr beeeee bö,   (A) 5

dll rrrrrr beeeee bö fümms bö,

   rrrrrr beeeee bö fümms bö wö,

      beeeee bö fümms bö wö tää,

         bö fümms bö wö tää zää,

            fümms bö wö tää zää Uu:

erster teil:

thema 1:

Fümms bö wö tää zää Uu,   1

        pögiff,

            kwii Ee.

thema 2:

Dedesnn nn rrrrrr,   2

       Ii Ee,

          mpiff tillff too,

                tillll,

                    Jüü Kaa?

                  (gesungen)

thema 3:

Rinnzekete bee bee nnz krr müü ?   3

            ziiuu ennze, ziiuu rinnzkrrmüü,

   rakete bee bee.   3a

thema 4:

Rrummpff tillff toooo?   4

CHOOSE YOUR OWN FORMALISM

BY

DAVID AUERBACH

I. ALL SQUARES RESIDE IN THE HUMAN BREAST

In 2007 game designer and Second Life CEO Rod Humble wrote a video game called *THE MARRIAGE*[1]. The player's goal in *THE MARRIAGE* is to prevent two squares from shrinking or fading out while circles drift around them. Moving the mouse over the shapes has curious but consistent effects on the size and transparency of the squares.

Its abstruseness immediately brands it an 'art' game. I don't have a problem with calling it art, unlike Roger Ebert, who raised the hackles of many a techie by claiming that video games could not be art.

There are two related issues that technology raises for art: nonlinearity and interactivity. Interactivity creates more possibilities for nonlinearity. Nonlinearity demands increased interactivity. Yet it is the formal implications of these two factors that cause the problems.

Humble's game wouldn't have necessarily exposed these problems, except that Humble rather guilelessly posted his interpretation of the game, which I excerpt here:

> The game is my expression of how a marriage feels. The blue and pink squares represent the masculine and feminine of a marriage. They have differing rules which must be balanced to keep the marriage going.

> The circles represent outside elements entering the marriage. This can be anything. Work, family, ideas, each marriage is unique and the players' response should be individual.

> The size of each square represents the amount of space that person is taking up within the marriage. So for example we often say that one person's ego is dominating a marriage or perhaps a large personality. [...] The transparency of the squares represents how engaged that person is in the marriage. When one person fades out of the marriage and becomes emotionally distant then the marriage is over.

> Your controls reveal the agency of the game. You are only capable of making the squares move towards each other at the same time or removing a circle by sacrificing the size of the pink square. You are playing the agency of Love trying to make the system of the marriage work.

Humble's symbolism is literal, rigid, and simple. It is more of an allegory than symbolism, relying on transient cultural associations (blue and pink representing male and female; 100 years ago this would have been reversed) to communicate the mappings to the user.

E

Yet there is also the non-symbolic sensuous aspect to the game, which exists apart from this particular interpretation. It does not necessarily relate to a marriage or to *anything*, as it is non-representational. Only by the contrived allegorical process does it get linked to particular concepts.

It is by now an old saw that form and content are not separable, yet we can still speak of a relatively clean separation of layers in THE MARRIAGE. Moreover, the difficulties in *joining* the layers without allegorical reductionism can appear intractable. There is no quick fix for the problems raised by Humble's game. Consequently I have much greater respect for Humble's bald and bold expression than I do for hackwork like David Cage's game HEAVY RAIN (Sony, PS3), which merited a rave review from Seth Schiesel in the NEW YORK TIMES:

> No single-player experience has made me as genuinely nervous, unsettled, surprised, emotionally driven and altogether involved as HEAVY RAIN, a noir murder mystery inspired by film masters like Hitchcock, Kubrick and David Lynch.

The faux hard-boiled dialogue reveals Schiesel's standards to be quite low:

> No one seems to know where all the rain is coming from. Scientists say it's unexplainable. But I can explain it. It's the angels above crying down at the travesty that is human life. Maria, I hope you aren't one of the crying ones. If I let her go, I'm scared I'll let myself go. Because if you stare into the abyss, the abyss might just stare back into you. Pain runs deep, but scars run deeper. If it's true what they say – it's blackest before the storm – then it's gonna be one hell of a storm. Buckle up. It's going to be a bumpy ride.

Much like Cory Arcangel's feebly hacked video game cartridges, HEAVY RAIN shows how much the bar has been lowered among the cognoscenti for anything reeking of technology and art. THE MARRIAGE, whatever its flaws, did not just regurgitate noir clichés. Its questions are the ones to follow.

2. CHOOSE YOUR OWN POSSIBLE WORLD

Consider a success of both interactivity and nonlinearity. Jason Shiga's MEANWHILE[2] is a comic book, or a hypertext, or a hypercomic, or an interactive story, or one of many other names. Published on the web in 2005 and as a book in 2010, it was finally made available as an iPad app in late 2011. It is a branching comic, where the reader can follow one of multiple paths out of many panels to make one choice.

XIII

The whole comic is very much a tribute to the Choose Your Own Adventure series, which entertained and irritated children with its unpredictable branching (turn left at intersection: become ruler of world; turn right at intersection: eaten by dragon). But beyond that, MEANWHILE is a commentary on the very idea of narrative branching. The plot has you, the reader, as Everykid, visiting a mad scientist's house and playing with his three amazing machines: a mind reader, a time machine, and the Killotron (which kills everyone on Earth).

The Killotron is Shiga's narrative coup. See, the mad scientist has rigged it to be an anti-entropy device: by, for example, having the machine flip a coin and only kill everyone if it comes up tails, he's able to selectively trim off the branches of the universe that don't have the organisational outcome he wants. This assumes that the Many Worlds interpretation of quantum physics is true, but within the context of the comic, *it is true*. Every time the Killotron flips the coin, two branches come out of the panel, one that merely says END; the other that has the result that didn't cause the machine to kill everyone on Earth and continues the story.

Shiga spins out complex refinements of this conceit by mixing in time travel, but MEANWHILE's brilliance lies in its ability to map a particular account of quantum physics on to a well-known narrative paradigm. It is an ingenious analogical manoeuvre, but a very formal one: Shiga has to twist physics a bit to get the concepts to line up properly, but the result is satisfying to grasp in the manner of Borges or Stanislaw Lem when they do line up.

Yet there is a limit here: Shiga's achievement cannot be easily replicated, because it required finding a format and a content that matched up quite closely. The aesthetic beauty of the work lay in that analogy not having been made before. Altering the formal aspects of the story would ruin the correlation, while swapping out non-formal details for others would only produce a copycat work. Shiga has not started a revolution in Choose Your Own Adventure-style narratives (nor would he claim to have done so).

Hence a more general lesson: formal innovations are almost impossible to modify or repeat. This is critical to bear in mind, since the artistic changes which technology enables are formal.

3. AN ORRERY OF ERRORS

In the late 1980s, a number of academics based around Brown University's writing programme discovered the computer and proclaimed themselves the masters of hypertext. Promoted by postmodern novelist Robert Coover, these writers issued a handful of hypertext works and many papers about the genre and its possibilities, all marred by a lack of technical knowledge and the sort of hubris produced by academic insularity. The works themselves are still available from Eastgate Systems for $24.95 apiece, if you can navigate the 1990s–vintage site. (Most of these writers were none too keen about sharing their work for free.)

The writing itself ranged from overwrought to occasionally quite good: the best writer of the lot, Shelley Jackson, has rightfully become a well–known novelist. Not coincidentally, her hypertext work is less self–referential and less formalistic than others: PATCHWORK GIRL lightly uses a hierarchical collage-like structure to pay homage to Mary Shelley and L. Frank Baum. Technologically, it is not especially distinctive.

At the other end, a nadir was reached in Mark Amerika's HYPERTEXTUAL CONSCIOUSNESS 1.0[3], a melange of badly formatted text and self–important oracular pronouncements. Let us brush away such rhetoric as this:

> 'The birth of the new media is the ultimate triumph of Information Capitalism. We are all now properly encoded bits of data struggling to subsist in the dream world of material culture.'

> 'Well, yes, I agree. The rule in business culture today is to increase the experimental intensity. We can apply this to publishing by creating havoc among the book–people so that they feel they have to get wired.'

The much–vaunted hypertext revolution promised greater reader interaction and narrative fragmentation to match our wacky hyper–virtual world. As Coover said in a 1992 NEW YORK TIMES article called 'The End of Books': 'Fluidity, contingency, indeterminacy, plurality, discontinuity are the hypertext buzzwords of the day, and they seem to be fast becoming principles, in the same way that relativity not so long ago displaced the falling apple.'

In truth, the techniques were in essence no more than what a writer like Stephen Dixon had been employing in his earnest, unaffected fiction (FROG and INTERSTATE, for two) for decades, to say nothing of the more radically experimental writers of the Oulipo. Shorn of the technological clothes, hypertext works were poor derivatives of HOPSCOTCH and PALE FIRE.

Today, hypertexts live on most closely in the form of the Japanese genre of 'visual novels', which are lightweight illustrated stories played on a computer with a handful of branching points at which the reader can choose the direction of the story: in other words, Choose Your Own Adventure stories. The theorists have not been rushing to claim these visual novels as their scions.

E

Literature has reason to be embarrassed next to music. Music was quite forward-looking when it came to technology. Composers like George Antheil had been working with electronics from at least the 1920s – possibly earlier if some of his eccentric mechanical monstrosities count. Today composers and performers regularly use laptops with signal-processing software more powerful than anything studio professionals could use twenty years ago. Landmarks such as Xenakis' *LA LEGENDE D'EER*, Karlheinz Stockhausen's *KONTAKTE* and *TELEMUSIK*, Pauline Oliveros' *BYE BYE BUTTERFLY*, James Tenney's *COLLAGE #1 ("BLUE SUEDE")*, and the *œuvres* of Pierre Schaeffer, Pierre Henry, Daphne Oram, Laurie Spiegel, and Francis Dhomont fill the twentieth century with technological and musical innovation.

Ah, you say, but music only consists of sound! But the difference of semantic content is not enough, since visual art, even at its most abstract, did not take up technology any more quickly than literature. What was it about music that made it so amenable to technology?

The answer is one of formalism. The past centuries of Western music had established a vocabulary that was quite precise: tone, volume, tempo and entire musical structure were expressed in fairly precise and often discrete terms. Though performance and interpretation allowed for much variation within a given score, these variations were comparatively minuscule compared to, for example, the variation in meaning of a single word of English or any other language. Many of these musical strictures were broken – sometimes quite methodically and exhaustively – over the course of the twentieth century. Crutially, they were there to be broken.

For all the adventurousness of the literary modernists, they were not faced with anywhere near as rigid a formal structure as musical modernists. Joyce, Proust and company did not abandon narrative in the way that Schoenberg and Webern abandoned tonality. Jackson Pollock and Willem de Kooning did not abandon shape and colour in the way that Xenakis and Stockhausen abandoned the musical line. This is a consequence of music having a far more formal and constricting tradition than those other forms. The closest literary analogue, that of metre, stress, and rhyme in poetry had long lost any dominant hold over the use of language as an art form.

Technology, which requires precise, formal regimentation of its content, could only be integrated into a system that was already sufficiently formalised. Music met this requirement, but language and literature did not. The formal manoeuvres of the Oulipo held fascination for many, but did not and could not point the way forward, for their techniques presupposed a formalising and limiting of language's use: for example, 'n+7', which replaces every noun in a text with the seventh word following that noun in the dictionary.

Emotional content may still remain: Oulipo novelist Jacques Roubaud's *THE GREAT FIRE OF LONDON* captures the pain of a loved one's death through its retreat into such manoeuvres. But it is more precisely a metaformalist work, a work about the use of formalisms rather than formalism itself.

4. THAT ISN'T IMPORTANT.

WEST OF HOUSE
You are standing in an open field west of a white house,
with a boarded front door.
There is a small mailbox here.

These are probably the most famous words of any text adventure, a genre also known by the more highbrow term 'interactive fiction'. The prototype for all future games was *COLOSSAL CAVE*, made in the mid-1970s by William Crowther and Don Woods, but it was a group of MIT students a few years later who created the better-known *ZORK* and founded Infocom, the company who dominated the text-adventure market until it died in the late 1980s.

The seeming miracle of text adventures was that they appeared to understand English, albeit a restricted form of it. The player could issue imperative commands in reasonably ornate English and stand a good chance of the programme understanding it. A sample Infocom transcript gives the general form, with player commands in capitals:

IN SPACE
You are floating in outer space just 'west' of your spaceship. A tiny asteroid lies below you.

>INVENTORY
You are carrying a plasma grenade, a pink feather duster, and a radium-powered radio.

>GO DOWN

ON AN ASTEROID
This is a godforsaken hunk of rock with nothing to recommend it. The horizon is deceptively close, forming a craggy circle around you in every direction.
Your rocket ship is floating a hundred feet above you.

>WALK EAST

OTHER SIDE OF THE ASTEROID

Your short hike has taken you to the other side of the asteroid, which is as ugly and barren as the first side. A human is tied to a stake here. Nearby, a tribe of rock-creatures are foraging around for chunks of ice. They obviously intend for this poor fellow to be frozen at the stake. Not surprising, considering how much rock-creatures love a good frozen steak.

>ASK THE HUMAN ABOUT THE ROCK CREATURES

'Thank the great red spot of Jupiter! A fellow human! Get me outta here before those rock-creatures turn me into a human popsicle!'
'There's some nice ice over here!' says one of the rock-creatures in a typically gravelly voice.

>EXAMINE THE PLASMA GRENADE

The deadliest weapon this side of Pluto, a plasma grenade is activated by pulling the pin and throwing it – as quickly as possible – at the person or thing you intend to turn into very tiny sub-atomic particles. One of the rock-creatures stumbles across some particularly frigid frozen methane, and scrapes its stony claws together in delightful anticipation. 'By the molten pools of Mercury, hurry up!' says the human at the stake.

>PULL THE PIN

The pin slides out smoothly. The grenade throbs with unleashed power. 'Isn't this enough ice?' growls one of the smaller rock creatures.

>THROW THE GRENADE AT THE ROCK CREATURES

Boom! The air is filled with a fine dust that one usually associates with vaporised rock-creatures. 'Good work! By the way, I am Umberto, from Ganymede. I pledge that I shall someday repay this debt. Now untie me, will ya?'

>UNTIE UMBERTO

You release Umberto from the stake.

>UMBERTO, FOLLOW ME

E

'You bet!'

The comprehension was, however, something of a ruse. Player commands had to be in one of only a few restricted grammatical forms, most of them variations on [VERB] [OBJECT] [PREPOSITION] [OBJECT]. Only a limited number of contextually relevant objects would be understood.

Once the player agreed to this restricted framework, however, a great deal was possible. At the genre's height, Brian Moriarty's *TRINITY* was able to mix magical realism with a story of the first atomic test to nightmarish and haunting results. The assignment of agency to the player, requiring them to type in verbal commands to move the story forward, produced a different sort of involvement than had previously been possible, and one that remains different from clicking with a mouse or using an Xbox controller. Yet the restrictions on player interaction stymied many traditional authors who engaged with the form: Robert Pinsky's *MINDWHEEL* and Thomas Disch's *AMNESIA* were not especially successful entries, though Disch's sadism toward the player (rather than toward his characters) made for a singularly frustrating game, intriguing if not enjoyable.

The arguable pinnacle of interactive fiction came many years later, in 1998, with Andrew Plotkin's *SPIDER AND WEB*[4]. By that time, the form had been revived by fans, many of whom had played the games as children or adolescents, and could now make games unencumbered by commercial considerations. Plotkin knew the history and the technology of the genre inside out, and the genius of *SPIDER AND WEB* comes from its many subversions of the form itself.

Chief among these is that the player is not playing out the story, but is participating in a telling of a story under hostile interrogation, and player commands that do not 'tell' the story to the interrogator's satisfaction cause the story to rewind until the player 'tells' the story to more convincing effect.

END OF ALLEY

It's a narrow dead end here, with walls rising oppressively high in three directions. The alley is quite empty, bare even of trash. (Your guidebook warned you: the police are as efficient about litter laws as about everything else they do.) You can retreat to the south.

A plain metal door faces you to the east, near the alley's end. It's firmly shut.

>OPEN DOOR
You can't see how.

E

>WALK SOUTH

You leave door and alley behind, and set off to see what else this fine city might hold.

– glaring light...

INTERROGATION CHAMBER (IMPRISONED IN THE CHAIR)

You blink away sharp edges of memory, and the dim walls slowly emerge into your sight once again. Dark metal walls and air uncomfortably cool. And cool metal bands around your wrists and feet and forehead.

He leans forward over his desk, through the glow of his monitors and controls. Impatience tightens his face.

'Don't be absurd,' he says. 'You're no more a sightseer than the Old Tree in Capitol Square; and if you'd had enough sense to walk away from that door, you wouldn't be here. You don't and you didn't and are; we caught you. And you're going to start by telling me how you got through that door. Do you understand me?'

>YES

The man nods briefly – a man satisfied with the least important detail. He touches a control. Once again, a faint whine begins to drill through your temples.

END OF ALLEY

It's a narrow dead end here, with walls rising oppressively high in three directions. The alley is quite empty, bare even of trash. (You're sure the police are as efficient about litter laws as about everything else they do.) You can retreat to the south.

A plain metal door faces you to the east, near the alley's end. It's firmly shut.

>UNLOCK DOOR WITH LOCKPICK

The lockpick's status dot fades to pure green, and flicks steady blue.

The door slides neatly open.

The game becomes considerably more complex in its violations of the basic metaphysical principle of text adventures: that you are controlling a player acting in the world. The result is, as with MEANWHILE, quite stunning and elegant, yet SPIDER AND WEB requires far more paradigm knowledge from its player. It is impossible to appreciate, much less complete, Plotkin's achievement without familiarity with the structural tropes introduced by earlier games. Once again, the details of the plot (which is not particularly relevant to the discussion) and the prose are secondary in comparison to the formal methods at work.

In exchange for greater interactivity and a greater formal achievement (one that exploits, more than anything else, the epistemological gap between the player and the player character), the work requires specialised formal knowledge on the part of the player. It is the interactive fiction equivalent of twelve-tone music, except that the formal system has only been known to a handful of gamers, rather than a vast swath of Western culture.

Again, such innovations are not repeatable. Just as Schoenberg's twelve-tone system quickly exhausted itself after producing some stunning music, Plotkin's work has yet to be bettered in the fourteen years since its release, despite estimable efforts such as *Slouching Towards Bedlam* and *Make It Good*, which engage in similar formal manoeuvres to less impressive effect.

5. FUMMS BÖ WÖ TÄÄ ZÄÄ UU, PÖGIFF, KWII EE

As with text adventures' restriction of narrative and language, other attempts to formalise language for artistic purposes have been made, such as the Oulipo. But semantic meaning is too tricky a monster to formalise, and so the most fascinating – and for the purposes of technology, most promising – formalisations have been achieved by abandoning the notion of sense altogether and treating words as sounds, which attempt to turn language into music. Meaning cannot be formalised, but phonemes can.

The Dadaists explored 'sound poetry': Hugo Ball, Kurt Schwitters, and Tristan Tzara abandoned any sense of language for pure explorations of (Indo–European) syllabic excess. In the hands of a skilled performer such as Eberhard Blum, Schwitters' *Ursonate* is lovely and musical.

Among writers, one influential figure looms large: Gertrude Stein. Was she the first $L=A=N=G=U=A=G=E$ poet, or the first Objectivist (in the sense of Louis Zukofsky, not Ayn Rand)? Stein's flat prose, cleansed of allusion and abstraction, opened up the possibilities for literature as a narrative yet non–representational force, but at a terrible price, which was the loss of easy access to conceptual force. Abstract concepts now could only be reached with the same difficulty as music, but without the legacy of music's power to invigorate, move and soothe.

Stein and the Dadaist sound poets are clearly the most fundamental influences on the movement Kenneth Goldsmith lumps under the heading 'uncreative writing' in his book of the same name (2011). Unfortunately, much of the work Goldsmith cites suffers from two mortal sins: lack of discrimination and lack of knowledge.

E

Goldsmith, who deserves plaudits for running the invaluable avant-garde archive UbuWeb, enthuses equally over Louis Zukofsky's *"A"* and Andy Warhol's *a* without making it clear that one is a gorgeous poetic assemblage and the other a numbing array of druggy prattle. A certain lack of discrimination can be useful in curating, to avoid cutting too narrow a swath in archival work; but in criticism the attitude is harmful. Promoting Warhol's writing and SMTP email headers as literature will prevent most dilettantes from ever reaching the vastly more worthwhile Jaap Blonk or Henri Chopin: avant-garde has never entailed an abdication of standards. Such standards are never absolute, yet we have never managed to do without them as a means of explaining and prescribing our differential responses.

But it is Goldsmith's technological ignorance that is a more germane problem. He confuses DOS and Linux, reads line numbers as code, and mistakes files for their contents. I can already imagine the response: these things are to be appreciated naïvely, as art. Yet to do so is to ignore any possible meaning of technology in our world in favour of its incidental surface appearance. It echoes the conceit of the older hypertext authors that they need know little more than HTML in order to grasp the impact of technology on art. The question of knowledge is necessary because worthwhile art will only come of such formalisms from people who know them inside and out.

6. FORTY-NINE SHADES OF SHIT

There has been quality work in parasemantic literary frameworks. In 1961, Oulipo writer Raymond Queneau created a work called ONE HUNDRED THOUSAND BILLION POEMS by creating ten possible versions of each line in the same rhythm and rhyme scheme, such that any combination created a proper sonnet. In creating his hundred thousand billion sonnets, Queneau had to sacrifice something: semantics. Very few of the resulting poems 'make sense' in any commonly understood meaning of the term, yet the sonorous effects and hints of sense they produce are evocative. The audience for mostly senseless aesthetic explorations of linguistic phonemes is likely to remain fairly limited, if only because the purpose of such aesthetic explorations is already subsumed under the category of music.

It is not semantics that produce such clunky marriages between art and technology. So much of Goldsmith's uncreative writing shows the abdication of sense to be of no help in producing good art. The clunkiness is due to the lack of a well-defined formalism for them. Character, plot, and meaning can be regimented as explicitly as musical pitch and duration, at the cost of nuance and ambiguity. These

E

frameworks do not currently exist in any dominant form. Shiga and Plotkin adopt existing genre tropes as a way of restricting their scope of meaning and making their formal innovations easier to grasp.

We are living through an interstitial period, in which we are seeing the creation of a large number of formally restricted narrative systems that can then be varied and subverted in formalised ways. The world is too large for one system or set of systems to dominate, but within a particular subculture, people will internalise these systems as poets used to internalise metre and rhythm (and, at least in a few subcultures, still do). This will entail the quantification of narrative, character and even theme to a near-mechanical degree, in much the same way that baroque music permitted strict formulas allowing Vivaldi and Telemann to write thousands of works, while after throwing away such formulae Beethoven could only manage nine symphonies.

One already sees such manifestations in the glut of vampire novels, fantasy novels, science-fiction novels, romance novels, and so on and so forth. As subcommunities of fans blur the lines between writers and readers, the emerging standards will more closely reflect the attitudes of these communities' members. Somewhere around the five-thousandth iteration of *TWILIGHT*-cum-*FIFTY SHADES OF GREY*, we could well see something of quality emerge, just as Alan Moore was able to reassemble myriad tired superhero tropes into the far more substantial *WATCHMEN*.

The problem with formalism is that it produces art that grips life only tenuously. Artificially sequestering an explicit set of concepts, such art performs magic on them, but magic that removes itself from the world that created those concepts. The ethical sense, the psychological sense, the human sense may go missing. So it is with *MEANWHILE*, *SPIDER AND WEB*, and even *WATCHMEN*: their achievements are not primarily those of human feeling, though we may feel touched by them. The attachment of sentiment to formalisms, like the feelings we have on hearing Beethoven or Joy Division or Britney Spears, are a matter of gradual cultural training. We are currently in the process of retraining.

[1] http://www.rodvik.com/rodgames/marriage.html

[2] http://www.shigabooks.com/interactive/meanwhile/01.html

[3] http://www.grammatron.com/htc1.0/wicked.html (Netscape 3.0 or higher required)

[4] http://eblong.com/zarf/if.html

E

IKEBANA

BY

CAMILLE HENROT

IS IT POSSIBLE TO BE A REVOLUTIONARY
AND TO STILL LOVE FLOWERS?

You start by loving flowers and soon you are seized by the desire to live like a property owner, stretched out lazily and reading French novels in a hammock set amid a magnificent garden while being served by obsequious servants.
LENINISM UNDER LENIN, MARCEL LIEBMAN

¶ Associating the ikebana, or collections of flowers, with collections of books is a way of making a connection between natural and cultural languages. In so doing, a space is made for some language that might surpass the traditional dichotomy of intellectual and decorative art. In my opinion, the reflections induced by literature, philosophy, or anthropology are an integral part of the everyday life and are, to a certain degree, 'decorative objects' in the sense that they create a stimulating and soothing environment.

¶ An ikebana is both an assemblage and a minimalist form (opulence expressed in a handful). The bouquet is a 'monad', an ensemble of fragments that reconstitute a world, and the image of the coexistence of uprooted elements. International commerce spirits these flowers all over the world; they sometimes disappear from their original territories to proliferate elsewhere.

¶ The minimal bouquets recall traditional ikebana, the abundant ones recall Western bourgeois flower arrangements.

¶ The cuts are sometimes drastic, imparting a feeling of frustration or lack, and so paradoxically reinforcing the synthesis performed by the ikebana, for which each individual element is a part of the whole.

¶ I've mostly used books that deal with our relationships to subjectivity and alterity, books that deal with exoticism, the projection towards an elsewhere, disillusion, the cult of authenticity, and the fiction in which it results.

¶ The problems and questions of anthropology make me think of those proper to romantic encounters, with the misunderstandings, the expectations, and the disappointments they breed – which is also the great preoccupation of literature.

¶ By making use of an oriental tradition, I hope to show the connections between natural language and cultural language while breaking up the hierarchies that idealise the language arts and underestimate the everyday arts in Western culture.

> The strange, mysterious, perhaps dangerous, perhaps saving comfort that there is in writing. DIARIES, FRANZ KAFKA

¶ The ikebana tradition is bound to the idea of an object soothing and consoling the soul.

¶ According to the Japanese legend, when Princess Izanami died, her subjects began to decorate her burial site with flowers so as to 'comfort her soul'. Contrary to occidental art forms meant to ward off existential angst – art that strives to resist the passing of time and attempts to take refuge in immutability – ikebana, which are meant to provide solace before death, are paradoxically short-lived objects. What's more, ikebana require a great deal of care: the flower arranger's state of mind is considered to be a decisive factor in any arrangement, as ikebana are taken to be expressions of their creators' thoughts and feelings.

¶ These two aspects of ikebana, its consolatory function and its evocation of thought, reminded me of the role that literature has often played in my life. Language, reason, and literature were considered remedies for the suffering soul from antiquity until the seventeenth century.

¶ The appropriation of a cultural language that does not belong to me results in misunderstandings and inventions. Even though it is positioned within a non-traditional strand of the art form, my ikebana practice is bound to include serious misinterpretations and naïveties – this relationship to error is crucial to the project and is one of its subjects.

[Text in collaboration with JACOB BROMBERG]

.

STUDY OF LENINISM UNDER LENIN
BY MARCEL LIEBMAN

STUDY OF ERRANCES (WANDERINGS)
BY LI XUN

STUDY OF A NEW REGION OF THE WORLD
BY EDOUARD GLISSANT

STUDY OF LA JEUNE PARQUE
BY PAUL VALÉRY

STUDY OF LIFE: A USER'S MANUAL
BY GEORGES PEREC

STUDY OF DIARY: HOW TO IMPROVE THE WORLD
(YOU WILL ONLY MAKE MATTERS WORSE)
BY JOHN CAGE

STUDY OF L'ÎLE DE PÂQUES
BY ALFRED MÉTRAUX

II

DORIS LESSING   CARNETS   D'OR

les immémauriaux
(victor segalen)

Afrique
Fautène : LEIRIS
(ajouté Alpinia)

white sl
m. sho

el-shap
consid
haped
s remir
f the fir
additio
tire sur
ip, bri
necked

ight tar

almost
ymboli
e remo
front
ntical and completely flat.

→ le lij dans la vallée
(Balzac)

...lrush and Japanese yellow water-lily in a white vase

...he technique for arranging wild-growing water plants permits more freedom of placement ...an that applied to cultivated growth. The technique of bending stems to form interesting ...es is used in arranging non-realistically. The same technique may be applied to ...oduce an appearance of wind-driv...

SENT

BY

JOSHUA COHEN

I. THE BED

BEDS ARE MADE OF TREES, and coffins are beds with lids. Death is sleep
without bottom. Its nature silent and consciousless and densely dark——

Imagine you are walking through a dream. But your dream is not just that, not
just open. Your dream isn't just one big grey open scape of mist you can step into,
you can walk anywhere through, stick a hand or arm or leg into and just wiggle
anywhere, no.

There are obstructions, even here. This is a dream with obstructions.

And so it is real. So it is real life.

You are walking through the forest but you cannot walk straight, you have to
walk where the forest says you can walk, around the trees that tell you Here and
There and Here. If straight is your goal you will have to go crooked. If crooked is
your goal you will have to aim crookeder. No, better a fairy should tell you, some sort
of dryadish creature: *'If straight be your goal you must go crooked. If crooked be your path
go forth and crook.'*

Yes, fairy. Yes, cretin sprite.

I am a woodsman. A forester. No. You are a woodsman. You are a forester. No.
Shake the tree. Uproot the roots. He, yes, he is a woodsman, he is a man in the woods.
He is thick like wood and brown like wood and nothing about him is green. He has
a bark beard. Knots for eyes and knots for ears and a knot for a mouth but while
walking he is silent. His wife he has left behind in their hut. From there, noises. Their
hut is made of trees, is made of tree, unwindowed. She lies on the ground expecting a
child. This would be their first. New leaves, new leaf, a child shaped in lobes with a
stem between the legs. She lies there in labour, lies on the earth belaboured, olid and
fat. She screams and screams and her eyes are angry. (He needs to move quickly.)

Fairies? *'You need to move quickly!'*

Thou spirits of lilim and such? *'Hurry, hurry fast!'*

He must build her a bed. He must build her a bed she can give birth in. And it
must be built well so that the birth will be well. But he has to do this soon, has to rush.

His ax has a name but no one will know that name. That name is a secret unlike
the name of his child that everyone will call him or her, he is expecting a Him. The
axname is secret because that is the name he calls when he needs the ax's power. The
ax was smelted especially for his father, with magical powers that his fathers believed
in and that he, the child of his father, believes in occasionally. But he also wonders
occasionally why an ax should have an axname like a child has a childname but the
ax's name secret, and there is an unease in that wonder that he does not understand
fully or want to. (Enough to know that the ax is sharp, though he's not sharpened it
since he was married. Not a whet since he was wed. He has cut hairs with it, though,

F

his, his wife's, he's cut with it the throats of hairs and the limbs of wild game and is not worried.)

The seed for the tree came on a whistling wind when God was new or the fathers were gods or when there wasn't much of a difference between them—it was blown in on the wind and then the wind stopped its whistling and there the seed fell and became planted with the force of its fall and was watered with raining. Weather, nothing more eternal than the weather. The woodsman was not a godtype, he couldn't have been one even if eternal. He was ugly and fat and short. 'O God Above [but this was just a thing he said] I am ugly and fat and short of haft!'

'But my ax is strong.'

The tree grew to be an amalgam of trees. A composite of marbled meats thick and dark under a bark. When struck, splintering like a muscle stretched apart. As a tree it was the widest but most stunted like him so he chose it and cut it because it was like cutting himself, which is what a child will do, he will cut you. Imagine you chopped open a tree and inside was a very small tree. That is what it's like to be human. To be both conscious and conscious of one day not being—and so we seed another.

The tree—which had been rained upon by centuries, its shoot trampled by armies invading and the sport of the hunt, having shaded picnics with Mama and lovers around its expansive trunk graffitied with the endearments of pocketknives and quivering arrows—took only an afternoon in which to fall, after which the woodsman dragged it through the woods under the lush green eyes of its upright fellows, shedding leaves shaped like tears and hearts and leaves back to his hut where he left it in the clearing, just outside the door. He did not go in to greet his wife, the sounds of her shrieking told him she was still alive and had not birthed yet. He did not need to go in, did not need to hear her shriek, already knowing that all would be well, that all would be Male: in the woods he'd buried a hunk of the dung he'd squatted for in the rough hole left by the uprooted tree, in order to propitiate (thank) the forest powers.

And though he did not believe in those woody powers anymore as his father had believed in them, and though he told himself that he often enough did not believe even in God anymore, still he squatted in pressure and heat and left in gratitude what he left—a stillborn blackish coil.

Then he made the bed.

But I should tell this story the way one should tell this story to someone who has never made a bed. When you tell this story to a fellow bedmaker you just say, He made One!

What did he do? he made a bed (not with sheets but with wood and nails), what kind of bed? a big wood bed he nailed—nevermind how, you whose beds at home

F

be unmade, nevermade. Nevermind the chop chopping, the lathe hump of knots to flatness and the plane, the planing. Nevermind those nails, which in days of yore my little squirty grandkids you had to make yourself, not buy, you couldn't buy them. He made the nails from out of dug earth, fingerdug——but there'd be no need to tell this to a nailmaker. Or to a fellow storyteller. Fill it in yourself.

There, the bed is done.

I will next explain its symbols.

'Please explain. . . .'

To begin with the bed was built and was built plainly given the haste, and babies were birthed upon it, but then over the years in his rare eventide leisure the woodsman would carve into the bed, would make carvings into the footboard of the bed, and into the bed's headboard too, with that selfsame ax held nearer the blade and then his practiced knife.

On the footboard, the lions he carved represented the strength of lions. The four bedposts he topped with carvings of antlerlike crowns represented authority. Or they might have signified majesty instead, we're not sure and neither was he, guided by hand and whimsy. Yet again the entirety might only have represented 'Representation'.

On the footboard he carved swords and fearsome wings that might've been of eagles or ravens if they had to be of something, something flying and not abstract. And he carved lances and bound sheaves of wheat but perhaps it was not wheat because who could grind it? who could grind wood and taste of it and think, wheat? That would be magic! That is the magic of saying This is That, of saying Here is There but it's not *but it is,* and that is poetry, which is a kind of art!

The woodsman carved into the footboard's wood a shield and a helmet and a pike and a mace, he carved a wood wolf, he carved wolves, carved a wooden steer, a stag and lamb, antlers, antlers more and more ornate, a boar, a bear. This was all hopeful, this was wishful, in a sense——this heraldry coming before the family to be heralded was finished. The woodsman, late at night, unprepared for sleep, was inventing the insignia for his family before family he had, because one daughter is not a family and neither are two daughters, but three daughters like in the olden stories, one pretty, one smart, one stupid and plain, are a family and then a son, who ignored the bed because he was too busy building his own life——he was too busy building his own life plainly and then, once finished, decorating it with ornament: with children of his own, grandchildren of his own.

The woodsman's son never noticed the bed, being too occupied growing his fortune, taking ore from the mine he worked in and piling it up, ore into ingot, into a huge new house with vast windowed rooms and whitewashed cabinetry with a silver filigreed tea set including matching kettle and minuscule handled bathtub for cream and bronzepotted rubberplants that grew to outlandish heights and editions of books in foreign languages that were about sex but served their women readers morals at the end, and he only used his father's shack as a shed for his wife's pampered, preciously fed livestock and, subsequently, for his newly acquired telephone the elaborate size of the automobile just then being invented but an ocean away that no auto could cross.

And this son, who worked his way up through the mines from working down in one up to soon managing the one he used to work at, eventually had two sons of his own and the older son one day looked at the headboard of the bed they kept for the family's babies to sleep in and for the importuning use of visiting relations and guests, in the rarest moment of Sunday repose looking at his grandfather's carving on the bed's headboard of a man among trees and saying to himself then aloud and in quotes, 'I see a man among the trees. My grandfather carved into this bedhead a scene of himself going out among the trees to cut one down to make of it the bed my father was born in. It is no more difficult than that, yet neither is my life. I have married well a landowner's daughter and, like my father before me, have worked in a mine and now manage the mine my father managed, my life has been work, not as much work as life had been for my father or grandfather, but it has been a success because of them, their sorrows.'

His brother—who was younger, a redskinned diminutive regarded as unmarriageable, born late in their father's middle age—scoffed at what his brother had said and said instead, 'You have no senses besides your eyes, brother! You're made entirely of surface! This carving our grandfather carved on the headboard of our father's bed quite obviously depicts the peasant or workingman imperilled in a forest of giants—in a forest of towering landowners and Titans of industry like your father-in law—and he, the symbolic proletarian, is dwarfed by them, in their shadow he is dwarfish and inconsequential. Indeed, this carving must represent to us the coming war where the poor who toil in the fields and in mines like ours will revolt against the rich who own the fields and mismanage the mines and after that war is ended no man will ever be lost in the woods of another's exploitation.'

And then there was a war. And both brothers fought in it but on opposite sides, the older brother compelled to fight in time but the younger brother an eagerly early volunteer for the Revolution that came through their country like a flood and like fire. And though the older brother—that pressured conscript fighting on the side of the greedy landowners and factory management—died in combat with a bullet just a screaming kopek paid to one ear, the younger brother survived and was in his medalled survival happy to decamp to a smaller apartment when his family's house was nationalised by the State after that war of class struggle concluded.

And so leaving behind everything for the comfort of the State—the tables and chairs and loveseat for the State to relax in along with a footstool upon which the State could rest its feet if it would expropriate any feet—the brother wracked with

F

considerable guilt took with him and his nursemaid wife only the bed that was soon
to be their daughter's—their daughter who grew up tall and silently beautiful and
unlike her mother, who was the daughter of a Revolutionary mine secretary, was very
wellschooled, having been sent away to university in the capital city to study biology
and squint around with microscopes but for only a year before she had to return
home with another war, this time an international war beginning because it was time
for her to get serious about the future of building her country and life, which meant
marriage.

And she saw in the bed in her parents' house she returned to, the bed she'd
almost forgotten from childhood, in its headboard carved with the scene of the man
wandering alone amongst the wood trees at night—a symbol of sorts, though when
she was younger she could not define it or untangle the meaning of her sadness. Her
switching the radio off to better look at it long late at night, lying with her head of long
straight brownblonde hair mussed against the foot of the bed in the style of its wavy
grain, in her maturation seeing in the carving of the carverman lost amid the immense
trunks of trees a symbol for, yes, that was it, *existenz* (the university had given her
that foreign word as a dowry), for man's essential predicament in the universe, how
we are lonely and lost to wander among trees so immense as to be incomprehensible
around us, not sure how we got into the woods or how to get out of them if ever,
and she saw that that carved man—she didn't know he might be the carver himself,
her greatgrandfather—was actually all men and all women too, unfixed, inconstant,
errant in nature just like the boy she flirted with declaimed: 'On the branch bare and
lone / trembles the belated leaf,' a young man who wrote her extensive letters though he
lived just across the courtyard, who smoked cigarettes he rolled with great fast skill
and drank deeply from a flask and scribbled his own poetry with jetliner imagery and
attended the movies regularly (but he'd never hold her hand during the newsreels).

She married him when he came back from that next war alive, marrying
him because just as the only expression of wood is in its carving into a thing, the
only expression of love can be marriage. And if a man who should be dead lives,
then when he comes back from his war wounded—even if wounded in only his
youth—a monument should be erected to him. And there is no better monument than
a child—not wood, not even granite.

She took the bed with *them* as a cradle, moving it into their apartment they were
reassigned to on the outskirts of their city (the country's second city: this was the city
of culture, not the city of business, though in truth neither could lay claim to either).
An old inconvenient wooden bed hauled incongruously up to the eighteenth floor of a
prefab prestressed panel tower above a playground poured to harden around a gnarled
jungle gym and rusty teetertotter teetertottering, a shattered litre of milk frozen into
a purple skating rink in the light waned through the birches—it was the oldest and,

F

given years, only wooden thing in their apartment of metal things and, given another decade, plastic clothing and plastic plates and plastic bottles and plastic glasses.

But her daughter, her daughter of flesh and not of plastic, the daughter's daughter when she encountered the bed throughout her lazy childhood—sitting on its lapse as if a couch to watch across the armlengthwide apartment the television set no bigger than a keyhole decided that its headboard depicted no symbols or representations at all, that there was at base nothing to that headboard's carving but a man standing in the woods, nothing but a man on one hand and the woods on the other and one was in the other and surrounded by it and that was the way it was and would be forever and nothing meant anything or could be signified. This was what she concluded—she who did not know trees, she who could not identify which trees if any in particular had been carved into the headboard's wood that was of a type she could not identify either. She stared at it inattentively over Tokyo cartoons about undersea robots dubbed into sibilant Slavics and would think only that it was nice, the bed, that it was nicely comforting but also old and disgusting and a disgrace to the new that could not be afforded or even enough manufactured in the days when she sat on it painting her toenails with seagreen and white housepaint, affectionate tokens from the building's manager who was infatuated with her and sat with her in silence watching her read her tricolour femininka magazines and drinking with her tea with 'cognac' (which he'd also brought, provenance uncertain).

Watching the television she would, when bored with the programme or news, which was often because the programmes were always boring and the news was nightly a lie, turn to nap her kohlrimmed eyes on this bedhead and muse to herself as if making a programme inside her own head fair and uncarved, 'What is that man in that forest thinking, is he thinking at all and what is going on with him that he's in the forest to begin with?'

But more often, dulled, she'd say dully to herself, 'That is a man in the woods and that is all he is, that is a man in the forest and that is all he ever will be—he will never do any better!'

She'd say to herself, 'He will never get out,' as if she'd do any better, 'like me he is stuck!'

She was herself like wood this daughter but like deadwood because she'd been chopped from the roots of her life and left unwatered to wither and die. She was hardened like bark (those were the stockings she stole from a friend), but absent mostly as if without sensation, which is to say that to men she was attractive because inaccessible in her emotions, her life passed her by like the jungle scenery in the background of Tokyo cartoons, her eyes glozing into knots and her mouth into a knot and her clear skin was in the mornings brittle but furrowed and rough in a wild way as if she'd been lasciviously dreaming and once a man—the building manager

F

Blatnoy, a frustrated engineer who used to work in a warehouse but also on the side for extra money and goods fixed audio/visual equipment for the Politburo's connected (he connected them), he'd eventually become her husband spastic and fat in a camouflage vest its pockets bulging with tools——raped her not on that old wooden bed she'd inherited and used as a television sofa and outdated newspaper rack or on the newer metalframed bed in the bedroom she shared with her mother but instead in the kitchen where all political movements are birthed, him bending her over the plastictopped table then over the range, amid the greasy knobs she gripped as he left of himself inside her a puddle (but this had become a Kommunalka apartment, so rape went on while a lab chemist ate her cold supper in the hall, while the widowed librarian they were forced to take in last month accused in raucous tones the cosmetologist next door of toiletseat theft).

Her daughter that was made that day she gave birth to nine months later into 1989, not in their apartment——their apartment that was anyway no longer communal after her husband had managed to clear their cotenants out into other units in the building and, once they were finished being built, into neighbouring towers newly irradiating from the dusty grassless central square of the complex——not on her old metal bed and not on her older wooden carved bed either where even a mother as late as her own had once given birth, but instead in the municipal hospital in a hospitalroom with three other mothers and one doctor collectively pushing, pushing more. A flat bland brown building, the hospital, with curling edges as if it were peeling——like a propaganda poster from the wall of the sky.

The daughter she gave birth to, though she resembled initially a wad of chewing gum, grew up——her ridges stretching into shapely arms and legs, the bubbles in her inflating further into impressive breasts. She was to be a person of more plastics and faster cars, of more freedom. She would live to enjoy the openness and transparency of fallen walls and no dictators with birthmarks in the shapes of tropical islands on their balding heads telling you anymore what dates and coal production facts you had to memorise at school, while, if you had the money, there was travel available to such tropical islands and any movie or book you wanted was yours if you wanted it and even if you didn't it could be yours still, you could have any food and drink at any restaurant or club because you could hold any job and start any business and could say whatever it was you wanted to say——'Fuck my elected representatives,' 'Empathy is Evil,' 'World War II never happened'——it no longer mattered in any sense of mattering.

But to her for whom communication was not a juicy long letter written invisibly in citrus or milk but instead a quick click on a keyboard, *Dear New York! Dearest Turkey!*——to her for whom free and openbordered choice was not a matter of allegiance or belief but instead a test of her appetite or depravity, for her the bed kept

F

in the hall she used to sit on when she tied her shoes whenever she went out, the bed acting as bench under which she kept her shoes for them to sleep if they were tired, for her it was a bed and nothing else——in her childhood she'd hardly registered its existence, you would've had to have asked her, pointed it out to her and asked her about it——and the carvings on it were just that, carvings, it didn't matter what was depicted just that the thing itself was an antique, maybe, and did it have a value, could we sell it, where could we sell it and what kind of money could we get for it? For her the man there was a picture of a man and the woods there a picture of woods and the wood was wood with the value of wood and rather it was the value of the depictions that in her adolescence began to interest her——that a picture could have a value separate from that of its materials she was just becoming aware——when her mother by the year 2006 had gotten sick with a hardness and a rigidity like wood in her stomach and then in her breasts and regularly she had to go to the hospital again sunk in grass faded thick and long like the hair she lost and the weight and her colour, this time not to give birth again, not to foal even her tumours, but only to die——Which brings us to the purpose of our story. . . .

This story will not end as it began. No more trashy tellings like this, no more folktales. Here is a folktale that will end as a story, as a novel if we're lucky, but still nothing to compare to the audio/visual.

Better to just show the bed! Fairies! Better to roll around on the thing and hear it sing! O spirited sprites!

There once was a folktale, but its telling had been forgotten over the course of generations. One day, however, a story was written about a lost folktale. Does it seem that what had been lost is now found? or only, like bone chips and deer tracks, explained?

'Once upon a time there was a bed.' And it was old and slept on as if sleeping itself down through the generations. And the generations generated because everyone married to have children and some of the children were born on the bed and some of the children only slept on the bed intentionally or not in the midst of watching television or listening to dance records or reading, God forbid, reading, and the children were always young but the bed kept getting older. It was *falling apart* at its seams, at its supporting beams, its boards would creak and give with loose joints, with loose joists, its nails snapping in two. And the parents of the children became grandparents and they too were falling apart——like beds themselves, sleepers fit for the coffin's lid with splintered limbs and the feeling of an ax pain brought down between chin and chest, termite infestation in the liver.

With her mother cancered in the hospital and dying, this daughter who's young and beautiful, this skinny gracile sylph nymph left alone for week three of chemotherapy

F

invites over to the house the friend she'd met that evening at a popular pub whose theme was Dublin, 'the friend' who doesn't speak her language and is from another country but still has many dealings with modelling 'representatives' 'representing' 'many' 'regional' 'publications' and who before leaving his home in American Ohio maxedout a credit card on camera equipment, a light and a microphone to tape to it, which all he trundles up the steep stairs to her mother's apartment (her father, the engineer, had abandoned them both a while back under circumstances that even the most omniscient of narrators would blush at), hauling this gear with the help of his, 'the friend's,' local pardner, a parttime 'event promoter' who also drives their van parked outside and alternates, in their movies, his penis.

When the foreigner had made her the offer at that fancily priced Dublin pub that evening, she'd offered to his pardner who spoke her language as his own, It might be fun? and the pardner agreed.

If I like it in life, why wouldn't I like it when we're filming?

No reason, no reason at all.

Not wanting to befoul her mother's bed—which she lately thinks of as her mother's sickbed where the woman lies usually so pierced with thermometers in every pit and fissure as to vomit their mercury into the nightstand's drawer—she leads her guests to the television's bed, that old wooden heirloom she insists on in a moment, a moment of dignity when 'the friend' says, Fucking nice bed! I dig the carvings!

She sits down on the thing and he stands across from her an elasticised waistband's reach from her nose as they begin with their talking, the script they're scripting as they go along ignobly worthless and, I'm 16, no say you're 18, I am 22 years old and say, 'This is my first experience'—and suddenly, the rehearsal's spilling into the rehearsed as he holds her and presses his beery lips onto her he's taking off her clothing and putting his fingers into her and working around her clitoris with the knot of his thumb. Grk, grrk. Foreplay giving way to penetration as in he goes and out he goes and in, the noise from the bed overwhelming, its protestations offensively loud—her as amatory amateur and him as professional 'friend', they're fucking the bed apart, the bed will be fucked apart. Grrk, grrhk, with each motion of their fuck being filmed by the pardner who stands across from them in the hallway on a chair pinched from the kitchen then up on the windowsill with a pointed shoe like a crowbar prying at the door—coming in close to zoom in, then going farther away again for a wide shot, and closer, and farther, and closer, and far, with each motion the sound of the dying bed overpowering any sounds they'd make, even any sounds that could be overdubbed by them or pretending others in vanside postproduction.

The bed wrecked in its throes, the noise of its legs and spine as if the chatter of the girl's rickety bones—an agony of creaks, a brutish splintering of howls and gurgles—them going back and forth and back as the pardner with the camera, lights,

F

and sound, pulls in, pulls out, in again then zooms out on the fourhorned raging bed wobbling mortally, it has knees now, it's on all fours now as they fuck on all fours atop it, ripping out tufts of mattress hair and popping buttons like whitehead pimples and, though we never know her real name just her naked beauty (how when she's on top her tits turn dizzying circles, how when he doggies her her breasts hang down like lucent bunches of fruit, like lamped grapes the veins), though we never know her real name just what she'd told him her name was or what his pardner had told him, interpreting, when he'd asked her just like they'd rehearsed, 'My name is Moc' (practice it, pronounce it *Mots*), she perhaps knows his name, because 12:46 in 'the friend' shrieks—we can just barely make this out above the bedsounds—Say my name! Say my name, bitch!

But Moc the bitch does not respond, or can't (and only later does she speak again, garbling what she'd been told: 'It tastes so big, it feels too sweet,' i t.d.). Anyway the bed from their sawing atop it is too loud to hear whether she responds with his name or not—her mouth an unlanguaged vowel as he slams her once, pulls out, pulls her toward him again, a leg gives way, two legs give way and they're leaning against a hallwall and the wall's rughanging that's purple and gold and damp with sweat, with fluids his and hers in toecurled arabesques, and panting as he straddles the splintered wood and her and strokes himself off into her mouth and onto her face in splinters that are white and the trees are wet and white like in another season (the calendar in the background, tacked to the opposite wall, shows nature and says, in translation, *May*)—the trees, the trees, the trees are webbed with sperm.

F

II.COM/MOC

I.COM

THEY SAY IN THIS INDUSTRY you need a professional name because then it's
the professional who's guilty and not you, then the profession is at fault and not you or
your parents, your schools or the way you were raised.

This professional name—and no, it can't be as rudimentary or flippant as
'Professional Name'—becomes a sort of armour or shield, speaking in newer terms a
version of what this Industry in its more responsible incarnations requires: protection,
a prophylactic.

A condom, a condom for a name.

(Or else, consider it like you would an alias for the internet, an avatar that can
investigate realms that you with your own name couldn't. A safer way of being
yourself, by being someone else.)

And they say that one not particularly unique way of identifying this unique
professional name is: first name the name of your childhood pet and secondly, as
surname, the name of the street on which you grew up—in which case I'd be Sparkin
West 2nd after my parents' dog (that shepherd we had for only a year, though I was
also something of my doggie's dog), and a lane that subtly grids the wealthier suburbs
of Jersey, where my father sits wrapped in the robe of his disused urban planning
degree as the hypochondriacally retired founder of a successful addiction counselling
business and from which my mother, trained as an historian, commutes daily to the
city to edit the travel and health sections of a trendy magazine for women and men
who read like girls.

Which is how I've come here or why.

From now on, in accordance with accepted journalistic practice, I will keep
myself out of it. Kept distant, alone. He was no journalist but the son of a journalistic
mother who in middle age had capitulated to exposes on waxing and superfoods that
stop aging—and his assignment so vague as to be birthright.

Grow, change.

He'd heard different things, not from any pros who know but from hearsay, from
wasteful reading around the internet, clicking through the links.

He'd heard that his professional name should be, first name the last name of his
fifth grade mathematics teacher, de Vaca, last name the first name of his favourite
aunt, Diana—and so de Vaca Diana. Or else that he should use the first name of his
favourite brand of candy and as last name the full name of his favourite baseball player
who played for the Giants until getting enmeshed in a major steroid scandal—Berry
Berry Smackers Barry Bonds. That was what he'd do in school. He'd sit with
notebooks, filling them with pen, with pencil, with names. Of other people he'd rather
be, of other personalities. He'd sit with pen and pencil, gnawing their spans to match

the gnarled branches just beyond the window, wet with rain, saliva. Always a thigh warm against the radiator. Then Ms de Vaca, Mr. Heller (English), Mrs. Rae-Heller (social studies), would draw the shade.

He was a mediocre student, but in order never to work every degree had to be obtained.

College was enrolled on the other coast, expensively intentionally, though it was called a university, despite it being the only institution that accepted him.

It was May and all those not vicious enough to have found an offer to stay seaside went home to their agrestic Midwests, back to Mommy and Daddy, inferior internships, inferable jobs. And he was going back too, he was scrambling to pack the room into the U-Haul rented for the week—pick it up on one coast, drop it off with another franchise on the other.

He'd found a parkingspace too far from his door, down the block. Opposite the dogrun overrun that bright breezy Friday, the benches surrounding filled with profs and students who dressed like profs, standoffish admins lisping infidelities by phone and the hirsute homeless underliners of paperback books—he passed them sweating up and down the three flights from his room to the truck, down the block, each load he carried farther down. Weightlifters in the park, lifting weights, lifting weights, lifting weights in reps, in tight swimsuits, in reps. The busstop crowded with blondness for the beach. Hot and blandly still. Clear. That scape so different from this, so different from here. (But it seems this might be the incorrect approach.)

He laid the carpet down in the back, then the shelves and endtables and wobbly coffeetable and coffeemaker by the kitchen corner, above a low shelf kept always for his pan, his pot, his fork and knife, spatulation. He was drenched, wiping the hair from his face then stooping to lift, with the knees, with the knees, his body carrying the boxes and its boxy self—overdressed in sticky jeans, but all the shorts were packed—in sudden jerks, in spasms. Bicycles swirled around, walkers walked and runners jogged, a tanned xanthous man in the park, lifting weights, lifting. Everyone was light, was weightless, he felt, and only he was sulking, pale and big and bloatish, loading himself down in this lumbering truck—he'd become a mover, a slomover, a driver, a slodriver, he had no plans for what would happen at home or what he'd do with the degree he wasn't picking up. Media, PR. IT, finance. Generous options, given Mom's connections. This country should take only four, five days to drive—he and Mom were supposed to have their conversation come Friday next, graduation being that week too, he wasn't sure which day.

When he was finished clearing the room he sat on the bed wondering if he'd forgotten anything, but he'd only forgotten what he was sitting on—tedious, it couldn't not be overlooked—Ms Zimmer's bed, the saggy loaner.

He scooped through his pockets, the jeans dried rough and hot, felt the truck keys, found the keys to the apartment. He left them on the pillow but didn't leave a note, no paper——he'd coordinated his departure with Ms Zimmer's root canal appointment, giving dumb excuses about slots and fees, the traffic.

It'd been too soft a bed, it'd gone too softly on him, he smoothed it, smoothed the pillow too, he'd never had sex there, he'd stopped even having dreams.

He called his parents to say he was leaving——sure as he was that his mother wasn't home——left a message:

I'll be back soon, Dad, nothing special to eat, just make sure to make the sofa up downstairs.

He thought about just sending an email, then thought the better of it: he'd email them later, as reminder, forty-eight hours or so into his crosscountry drive——on a heartland signal wavering like grain in the wind, wavering then true, fixed and true.

What would he say then? what would be the Subject?

The man who invented email——sending messages from one computer to another——never revealed what was said in that first email ever sent. Unlike with the innovators of the telephone, whose testimony we have——unlike with the first man to swagger pithy on the moon.

What did that first email say? why did the inventor never tell us? Probably because that message was obscene. Probably said, 'Sveta, lover, I want to fuck your face off !' or, 'Daddy, why'd you touch me there?'

This was Illinois.

He'd been up all night so late that it was two nights——so this was Illinois. And had finally slept by dawn and woke by noon, undressed at his computer.

As he stretched a yawn his computer woke too, its screen confirming: he'd bought a ticket for an international flight departing in six hours.

Such are the problems you get giddily into when you have access, the situations brought about by life's late convenience——how convenient it is to be connected, modern.

His parents' credit card.

He checked out of the motel——as if his purchase on bliss couldn't be roomed anymore——found his rental, that cumbrous truck packed fully, got behind the wheel and drove toward Chicago——he was on the highway, he'd clung to the outskirts.

He left the truck in extended parking——one lot the same as another, or it's only that he's misplaced the number, his section, his row——there unburdening himself of his dirty bedding and dirty clothes, the corrugated boxes of incorrigible books, loose Registrar slips and Bursar receipts, the last days of being a student condoms optimistically purchased, bilingual dictionaries overdue, photographs of parents but none of friends, not that he wasn't into photography but that he had no friends. He had a wallet on his person, that abused credit card.

The check-in clerk asked, No luggage?

He said, No thank you, but the clerk didn't laugh, a mousy nondescript whose only pleasure was making hassle.

OK, description: her eyes were small and her vest was on too snug (he couldn't look at other women).

Then he explained, he had a girlfriend where he was going who had everything already: clean boxerbriefs his size, toothbrush and paste, multiflavoured flosses—all he needed was his computer, computerbag on his shoulder.

Imagine that truck, then, the back of it.

Open it, scroll up the rear door and what you'll find is his room, wholly intact, packaged just as it was: carpet sample put down first, then the shelves surfeited with shelfware, the two lamps on the two endtables below the two speakers installed one each to the high rear corners, the interstate miles of stereo wire, even the empty bottles he wanted to keep as proof, the winebottles, the beerbottles—proof of what? 80 proof, 90 proof—he'd hung a couple of frames on the truckwalls for art: one abstract, one not, a print of a celebrated portrait but he always forgets of whom (though 'a muse', she had to have been).

Still, he couldn't have slept there, couldn't sleep even in the bedroom's original setting. Not that he'd neglected it, just that it wasn't his. Ms Zimmer's bed, her spare, sitting back on the other coast in an otherwise stripped room, waiting for her sergeant son's disposal (after court, after a doubleshift policing Venice)—it'd been lying around her basement for years before she'd struggled it upstairs. She'd rented him the apartment, offering the bed only to rob him on utilities. He'd stolen the linens in revenge but then remembered they were his, he'd bought them, white on white. The mattress still pristine, the frame as unsturdy as it was the day he'd put it together —decrepit, a pall plot missing screws.

Now his last communication, after passing through Security—not that phone message he'd left on his parents' machine, but the email he sent from this airport halfway across, the tarmac tailgating the plains.

Crosslegged by the gate, he wrote, he typed:

Dear Mom, I've gone on assignment. Reserve me space in the spring issue next year.

Dear Dad, Hope your disability case goes well with the Port Authority. I can't think of a second sentence for you.

Sincerely, David.

He pressed Send.

Your message has been sent.

His message has been sent.

F

X X X

HE'D WANTED A DIFFERENT LIFE, a new life. Which should have been as easy as buying something. As simple as opening a new account. He'd wanted to make a new name for himself and the new password that would access his secrets would be ('preferably some combination of letters and digits')——no, no passwords. And no different names——no name at all.

Whole afternoons used to be as quiet as that Illinoisan motelroom was by dawn——once upon a time (childhood) whole weeks and even months passed by that satisfied, that ecstatically calmly, drugged on the horizonlessness of time, on his being alone and lazy and too young to know any better, before the days became broken up by access, noised by opportune technologies.

He'd been rockabyeing in a rockingchair, then on the bed, thickly rumpled. On that motel bed big and foreboding, as large as the room and as hard as the floor, a lump of carpet topped with a pillow as sharpcornered as a box. Through the window he saw the parkinglot, the truck, a smudge of moon, a muggy night, the window fogging. The bed was soundlessly elemental, like a boulder or tree grown up from the floor, from the fields, the soildark asphalt. The television could be turned on but no higher or lower than no volume on Channel 3——the remote control was missing.

He plucked an Apple——his. It had been a gift from his parents——for his birthday, for their having oblivioned his birthday——congratulating him on having been graduated from the age of being gifted. Whenever his parents gave him a gift it was so rarely specified what occasion it was for, often one gift would have to suffice for an entire year and then in one month, spring's, there would be this random, guilty superfluity of presents.

It was insufferable, their worming. His mother had deadlines and the internet (where she'd met her new friend, whose Manhattan condo she'd been staying at most weekends), his father had not having his mother and a phone that followed him everywhere (though only his addicts ever called and he didn't get out of the fridge much)——this was their remorse. His computer. Peel the screen away from the keys and all the letters glistened. It could spell *cultivar* and *calyx* and *stamen*, it could spell *exocarp* and *endocarp* and *mesocarp* and *pome*——it could spell *spelling* and *apple*, a-p-p-l-e, *apple*——all while circumscribing the cryptogeography of Eden, vegetarian recipes, porn.

F

The white box whirred as he began to waste——life the same as battery life, he couldn't be bothered to plug anything in, he was tired but wouldn't yet crash.

He had to sap the stress of driving——enough driving the trees and the roads, the rubbaged rumbling shoulders——this screen less boring than a windshield.

How could he even begin to map what was inside his Apple, its pulp contents? its seeds? On top of everything, on the desktop, there's a folder called *Davids documents* and in the folder called *Davids documents* there's a subfolder called *Sophomore_year*, which contains in itself subsubfolders called *Math* and *Science* and *Math_again* and *Science2* and *Language-and- literature-requirements*, which contains inside not a folder anymore or folders within folders like a Slavic doll nested one doll within another within another like they're pregnant already——that's what happens whenever a user turns his back and leaves them, even toys, alone——but files, files upon files listed and named and the names of these files are *Gandhi and Gandhi-one- more-time* and *Pilgrimsprogress* and *Pilgrimsprogress-final* and, lastly (alphabetically), *What activitees I did on my summer vacation*, which is a file, no, an essay, no, a paper from as early as fifth grade, which begins: 'What activitees I did on my summer vacation was to go with Mom to gazebo. We went sailing and I got 'severely sunburn,' the doctor said, then chickenpox also and laid in bed with vanilla ice cream, taking weird smelly baths . . . The End,' he actually wrote, 'The End.'

He sat out on the furthest bough of his Apple——leaned against the cold headboard, plastic, against the cold wall, the wallpaper testing its pattern of bars. He was a file called *Him* in the folder known as *Motel*——the motel's proper name lodged in the throat. Its decor was worse, inconsequent. A mess of burns, of stains——but who hasn't read motel descriptions before? who hasn't stayed in motels themselves? Any description would be extracurricular unless he could blaze another way, an alternate route——the green road branching from the red road, the main road always the red road smouldering down south into the black.

Imagine there is a God. Just imagine, you don't have to all of a sudden believe in anything and cut your scrotum or go bathe your head in rivers. Imagine to yourself that there's this omniperfect entity looking down upon us all, with eyes, with real anthropomorphic eyes, really looking. Now, imagine He's doing so from just above this motelroom, which is a rectangle of sorts, it actually looks like a screen——and there is no roof, God has taken the roof off Himself. You can locate our hero in the lower righthand corner. There, he's a dot. A forgettable pixel, the whim of a bawdy baud. You thought only a splotch of coffee, a sneeze's stain or semen. But him, picture him. Now, God or the motel's invisible management, take Your giant finger and place it over him, Your cursor. Place it directly above his face. Directly above and blinking. Click.

He opened *a window*——not an actual window onto Creationdom, just something

F

we call a window. An opening into a new otherness or alterity, not to make it sound any better than the depressing it was. Though it was good the motel got such good service——he was connected, stably online, for a fee. To be added to his bill. Spending so much money, so much of it not his.

He was tired of unfinishing delinquent assignments, tired of rereading homework done in a rush. He entered into the browser the address, which he wouldn't store in memory. Instead he'd stored it in his own memory and supplied it every time. Daily, often twice: www., the name of his preferred diversion, .com, which stands for 'commerce'——he pressed Enter, depressed, also called Return.

This site he frequented on select evenings and weekends and weekday mornings and afternoons loaded new vids daily, that's how they'd advertised at first, 'Tens of New Vids Daily,' then it was 'Dozens of New Vids Daily,' and then in flusher times (flush the fraught tissue down the toilet), just 'New Vids Daily Cum Check Them Out,' and sometimes he sampled those new vids while at other times he sampled the other vids he'd missed on the days he'd fructified with only one or two of the tens and dozens on offer. An incentive to, as the site's top teaser banner advised, 'Xxxplore.' None too brilliant but comprehensive, the site gave variety, moreover, it was free, he assumed supported by its ads: swinger networks popping here, loading there the freshest fleshlight sextoy (now phthalate-free), longdistance callingcards (Centroamerica).

We wish to communicate how guileless he was——there in that middling motelroom as in his dormer apartment, no expert, no connoisseur. He had experience but no discernment, and anyone who tells you that the more time you spend with something the more particular you get about it has never been stuck in a marriage to his parents, has never grown up a boy with appetites and television· more is only more of more and to invoke subtlety or fuss is merely to show fear in the face of glut——Jersey boys in neon motels are never intimidated, they're never afraid.

They just drop their pants (he dropped his pants). Stretched the underwear down——there's no concern for not being prepared, no worry as to whether or not he's ready. The computer is always ready, the internet's always open (he's never been unattracted to himself).

Bound by gridded paper, between panel ceiling and patchy carpet, he was as erect as the walls, as hard as the walls (telling someone how hard you are is to flatter yourself in lieu of claiming girth or length).

We shouldn't be so crude. Though we're sure whatever document we've opened, still unnamed, still unsaved, we're sure it won't be saved. *They-say-in-this-Industry.* Keystroke, stroke. Drag to trash.

When you're on that first page or window of the site, when you're in its Home, you're faced with a list of vids, and each vid is advertised, in a sense, by a still from the vid, a stilled scene from the moving scene to come——a freezeframe or screengrab, a capture.

If you like the looks of that single, practically measureless moment, you click on it and the still image loads into a moving image——the vid moves, *a movie* (we can't justify explaining this here, it just feels like it needs to be said——we'd rather not presume as to the depravity of our audience: Hello, Mom).

A taste is always given first, a still and silent taste, because if everything was sounding and in motion all at once, all the vids, you couldn't decide which One would gratify desire, you'd become confused, Mom, and the warmth of your breath would become the overheating of anger.

Her screengrab seemed unpromising——he didn't know why he clicked, maybe because even in the context of amateur porn, theirs, hers, was the most amateurish and he felt for that, not erotically, he felt pity. Even in still silence it came off as wrong, as wrongly incompetent. Fuzzy, unfocused. Angled oddly. The fan whirred to cool the drive, cooed. His mouth was dry, tongue heavy. It was a corner of her mouth then a swatch of smaller penis (onscreen all penises are smaller), a tracery of drool.

The room was dark. Nothing existed outside the spotlight of the screen——bluish, greenish, mucoid, queasily regorging——nothing existed outside the weakly fluctuant cast of its halo.

How could we remember any of the vids before her? how could anyone? She erased them, what deleted them was her apparition, her apparency. Though we might, like the virtual does, lie: we might say it was a big lips blonde that did it for him, or a shy spinnerette with tiny thimbleplug anus, we could say Latina mature with redblue hair and puffy nips for knees, we could say young teen hairlessness, Black Mama, we could fabricate forever. . . .

He was of a generation——no, bad word, bad habits . . . we're trying to say that everyone is our age now, even if they're not. We all grew up with this crap, we didn't know anything else——like Dad did, who masturbated to paper, to brownpaperwrapped magazines: pages glossy like lips, breasts shot verso, recto displaying recto, the navel that is the centrefold. Magazines not like the ones you work for, Mom——not fair that your son's father had to be your husband too (though Dad never mentioned sex).

Our generation doesn't have to hide anything under the bed, to secrete the forbidden in the closet, behind the shoes, behind the socks smelling like semen, the socks smelling like shoes. Instead ours is a practical pornography, with no awkward visits to newsstands or subscriptions to renew——there are no secrets, the entirety is acceptable. The computer sits proudly on the desk in plain day. There to help with the spreadsheets, with directions. We can just press a button and, naked lady. Press another button, another lady, nude. Point, click, penetration, it penetrates, it rewires your brain. You come to expect that all women take it up the pooper, take goop on

F

their faces and into their mouths and, swallowing, that they all do so voluntarily, with nary a complaint in rooms like this one: unlived-in-looking, filthily-linened, plywood-doored.

You—

You are not always a reader, you are occasionally a human. You are, often enough, a human who is not masturbating. There are other things to do with your hands.

Write. Type, type.

Write, *I want to be a writer.*

Write, *I am a writer now.*

As a human, ask yourself—would you describe, publicly, losing your virginity? Would you, Mom, freely detail the first time you ever had sex in love or how exactly your husband or boyfriend moans, what they say during sex in the throes, would you tell that to a stranger, would you make report, could you bring yourself to recall and divulge that night you faltered or conceived, that sensation—and here we're asking Dad now—of being inside someone for the first time bare, unsheathed, how that felt so wet and hotly illicit without protection?

If you know how difficult that is, to describe such feelings and to do so unabashedly, without scruple, then you know how difficult it would be for us to describe this—this vid, her sex in it.

We will not describe it, we cannot—describe her hair, her dense brownblack hair and thickly furred furtive eyebrows of same, the brownblack but also yellowish eyes their flicking lids, sorry, we won't describe them either. We will not describe her interview—brief because ashamed of accent and, he suspected, a deceiver in her answers—cannot describe her undressing, how slow it was and how methodical her removal of clothing to bare skin like a cashier she was meticulously smoothing one item at a time, folding each garment like a bill at the edge of that fantastic bed we won't describe that gave such horrid creaks when she threw herself upon it flat and splayed for his ravage, apologies, *it sounded like*—it sounded like—

We won't narrate the foreplay, what of it there was, first kiss the last, the same as the last. Won't detail the oral, cannot in fact put into words the oral eyes that flickered in and out of contact. With him, with the camera. That first push into her, through her, stop. The jointed sighing, sighing. Won't describe the swirl of breasts like clapping hands, as he—the man—pushed in and out, in and out and in. The two positions requisite then the third—missionary, her atop, reverse cowgirl leveraged canine from behind—the old bed's collapsing rattle. Couldn't hear her voice. Couldn't hear his own. Won't describe the sound as *wrenching*, a car crash of woods and metals. Then him, 'You like it you like it, what a pussy, say cum for me baby,' and her, 'Come for me baby, tastes too big, feels so salty'—two lines shot across the breasts we won't describe not even one, that dab on her tongue, collected in a dimple of her cheek.

The broken bed widelimbed, a dead huge hairball spider——we won't describe any of it.

That's the problem with the screen, you can't. You're always one step, but the crucial step, removed.

F

II. MOC

HELLO MY NAME IS MOC and today I have make my first sex on camera. Just for you @1stsexoncamera.com

Let's try that again, he said, just read the card he's holding.

The card? she asked.

Read it.

Hello my name is Moc and today I make my first sex on camera. Just for you @ first-sexy-on-camera.com

Try it again.

Hello my name is Moc and today I make sex with cameras. Just for you @ first-sexy-cameras.com

Say it com, not *cum*——do you know what that means?

Hello my name is Moc.

Can you stop? I asked you a question. *Cum*——don't you know what that means?

Com?

Yes.

No.

Cum means open your mouth and take what I give you. *Cum* means open your fucking mouth and take it.

Fuck?

Good. Do you know what the redlight means?

Redlight?

It means fuck. Means fuck till I *cum*.

Fuck means *cum*?

Very good.

Money?

How much I say?

You said 5,000 much.

That's what I said?

You said.

3,000.

That was their exchange——and, *Cut!*——unfilmed. But later they'd pretend they'd just met each other, when they began filming, when the redlight lit red.

O fancy pantsing you here, what's your name, beautiful? do you want to go back to your house and get better——*ah-vaynt-ed* was their pronunciation?

ON, we're rolling. . . .

Moc, 'the friend', his pardner holding the camera——having dealt with the lights and mic—holding the cuecards too, because the girls could never be trusted to remember: Say the website's address at the beginning, repeat it at the end, www., with shotwad slopping from your face.

They were just passing through.

Who are you? the girls would ask him, would ask the pardner, Who is he?

He'd answer, I'm just passing through. Hanging out. Hanging. As if a gunslinger from a Western, a drifting private eye. Doing the circuit, the stations, making passes. The tiny villages off the highway. Little tiny townlets far enough from the capital's allures. He could've been a bonafide desperado, a bonded dick—none of these women, these girls, had met an American before.

Have you ever met an American before?

She shook her head, they shook her head into smoky curls, into corkscrews—Say, No.

And though it was the same script every time, each fall was as unique as its fallen:

In each Location—as they called every town where they porned—the first thing they'd do would be to identify the raggiest regional newspaper, where were sold birds not yet caught and deceased grandmothers' furniture and preowned cats, the paper most people used to wrap fish in, to wrap trapped Rodentia for placement outdoors and severed limbs too, in the hope of reattachment—their ideal a paper that informed on local gossip while providing annual photos of the mayor in a goofy folkloristic helmet slaying a marionette dragon at Carnivaltime, this being the news most preferred. With papers like that rates were cheap for double columns in inksmudged colour and half or even full page spreads, but they always requested something small so as to seem special, unobtrusive—a small box relegated to the crossword's classifieds, a clue.

He and not his pardner, who'd always ask to place it himself, would place this advertisement and the ad would say: *We want girls 18 to 25. Must be nice.*

But it said all this in the wrong language, in this language—'the friend' didn't know the right language, he never would, the language things were in over here. That was the problem that was, at the same time, an asset—that he only knew how to speak what was not spoken too well by must be nice girls 18 to 25.

He was from—I don't know where he was from—Ohio, where his mother lived, say. He was big, broad and jangly in big fat stretched college sweats, always sweatshirts, always sweatpants (he didn't like zippers, he didn't like teeth). A whole wardrobe of that mottled blackswirled collegiate grey—a colour that exists nowhere in nature. He was a beerdrinker with a beergut like he'd swallowed a keg but also swollen all around—beerwrists, beerneck, beerknees. Eight countries' worth of change in his pockets. He wore sandals, never socks.

F

Strange——I was always hearing about the no socks whenever I asked about his looks——his toes were long, his feet flat, apparently he was bowlegged.

But I've heard other things that conflict.

That despite being baggy——'skin like a paperbag,' said one woman who introduced herself on a streetcorner on my first morning abroad, a girl he'd propositioned at a public pool——he was actually a trifle handsome. He was bald, not bald, balding, with black plastic glasses, with bluetinted metal sunglasses in the aviator style. Prescription, nonprescription. Never with a baseballcap, never without one, glasses resting on the brim, no glasses but a single studly earring. Hanging down from the cap a fringe of greyish white hair like an uneven row of incisors grown from the back of his head.

'The friend' always with a toothpick. 'The friend' never with a toothpick. The ladies asking, Who is *toothpick?*

I've also invented a lot, for you, for myself.

After his mother remarried——a soybean farmer——he moved in with his ailing father: Sandusky, then a suburb of Indianapolis, and then New York for two years for film school. His father paid tuition, incidentals.

Imagine, two years of incidentals: Central Park swanboating through springtime afternoons into one night stands with women from the same hall, from adjacent dorms, with divorced faculty who'd loan him keys to Harlem——the next mornings the endless circling for an uncrowded bagel brunch, before a mile of museums to trudge, jamming to gentri-fi in Brooklyn, gentri-lo-fi in Queens, buying skank weed in Washington Square.

And his face was said to be a square, though wrung loose, spongy, and he didn't shave that often, he didn't have to——he shaved down there more than he ever shaved more north. When it came down to it, he wore no underwear so that his erection poked its hyperactive contour through the sweats. Jingling testicular pockets stuffed with coin. His cut cock was as hairless as a tongue. And had a tongue's dimensions when flaccid. When it came down to it, 'the friend' had only one language fluently——this speech emerging slickly before the punctuating cash.

Whereas his girls had many languages among them: they spoke Slavics like Catholic Polish, irreligious Czech and Slovak, and Hungarian, which is not Slavic, and Orthodox Ukrainian and Russian, which are.

Moc——which was or is her name, whether it's a pornonym or not I didn't know then, I couldn't have——is a word common to all Slavic languages but with multiple meanings and in not two of those languages does it mean the same thing. In Czech, *moc* means 'extremely', 'very', or 'much', and in Slovak *moc* means that too, but it also means (I've been told, I have no way to gauge for myself) 'might', or 'force', while in Polish *moc* means something like 'might' as well, though I've been told it's more accurately 'strength', or possibly 'power'.

How do I look? they'd ask unclothed, disrobed from solo showers, embedded.

Look good? and, Good, 'the friend' would answer from atop her, or from behind the camera if he'd let Yury indulge, *Moc* good.

Men had used guns and fountainpens previously. They shot hot bullets into the mouth of the enemy or wrote vast scrolling poems to denounce their close friends—and this was how a life was destroyed. Several ounces of dun lead in the skull or O your politics are as ideologically corrupt / as an autumn without pears. And only memory would remain until the last remembrancer, he who squeezed the trigger or wrote the rhyme, had perished himself, his memory gone with him—but then they invented the camera and nothing would be forgotten again.

Moc was then—Describe yourself.

Use your fantasy, your imagination—your sister as model if sister you have.

As blackbrown hair with streaks of blonder dye like the markings of an insecure woodland pest runover by a van on a highway also striped like her hair, eyes bluewhite—but raptured with revelry's conjunctival bloom in the stills he took for his personal album, the tattered scrapbook 'the friend' kept in the glovebox, along with the maps, Yury's ammunition—just a barrette over 5', converted from the metrics she gave, 105.821 lb. the same.

In her purse was an apple, at bottom the tobacco from a broken cigarette like a crushed finger.

And her phone, stored in it the last number she'd dialled or that had dialled her. ('The friend' kept boxes of new phones in the glovebox too—a new number sometimes each village, sometimes each trip.)

Her wiping up with a towel—having dumped the phone and apple from the purse to locate her lighter—was the last shot in her vid. A light for that comminute cig. Or to spark the mortal kindling around her.

But then the lens fluttered its lashes, blinked its cap—and she wasn't there, she wasn't only there:

Moc wasn't at home anymore, Moc was home already.

Whereas 'the friend' lived in the capital. An expiscatory expat who'd recently sunk the bulk of his inheritance from his father's death back in Indiana (diabetes???) into a gorgeous old palace in the old city centre. Wainscot for the halls, bespoke boiseries for the rooms, faux chambres set with arched fireplaces like windows—windows to flame, to hell—pastel friezes arched above the doorways depicting either nobles hunting a stag or a stag running away from a band of men intent on pinning it down, forcing it to admit what it really symbolised—Nature, innocence or freedom, art thou Christ?

The stag ran around and around the rooms, above the doors, insouciantly gallivanting mantels, gamboling sills, threatening to shatter the rosette and tulip mouldings, the ceramic tiled stove. The parlour areas—there were perhaps three proper parlours plus two possible bedrooms he also referred to as parlours—he'd left flagrantly unfurnished: windy spaces canvased with renovation's remnants, plastering arras, blank tapestries of polymer sheeting.

Even the Master Bedroom, the only bedroom occupied, was bereft—just a sleepingbag strewn small on the floor like a leaf fallen from a crude fresco of trees (eastern wall through northern wall continuous). The bathrooms were highly ceilinged—with a stock of mints in each bidet—the hallways long and, since he didn't use any of the unreconstructed salons they connected to, utterly pointless. Only parquetry buffing the reflections of chandeliers—and of the screens on every surface: in the Master Bed, the Master Bath, suspended above the elevator doors, screens for screening, for televisionwatching and movies, screens for editing, for web support and maintenance, screens for power failures and backups (hooked to a somniloquent standby generator), screens for screens in banks.

The main entrance to all this flaunted an anteroom entirely empty except for a single tabling entity—a mediumsized chest or toppled armoire cluttered with par avion and torn aspirin packets—that he called the piano though it was, in truth, a harpsichord. He never played it but sat on its stool occasionally and when he looked at the stool and saw, instead, a steeringwheel, he knew it was to time to get moving.

He was hardly at this home, however, and so did most of his living, as he did most of his editing—his editable living—in transit. On the road. Always being driven by that swarthy pard with the spray of sesame seeds across his face—potentially a birth condition—and breath that smelled of 'pomace' (according to the dictionary of one interviewee—an evenbanged brunette with diacritic zits who contacted your correspondent about a week after he landed in-country—who gave Yury's name as İlgiz İrekovich, said he was partially Tatar and the father of her child).

Barrelling in that bloodred van (all the interview subjects mentioned that, as red as blood), from borders as illegible as signatures, to checkpoints blurry like their stamps. While idling at a crossing, the joke was: Where's the separate lane for the Americans? The guards kept the envelopes they were handed, sealed—they didn't need to be reminded of their lines.

From goatweed town to village, the farther away the better, the better chance at gullibility on the part, and it was a part played, of the girl. Same gist, different oblast. But never getting so far from civilisation—twin crowhaired Gypsy subjects stated that Yury had told them—that they'd lose their signals: their phone reception, a dependable internet connection (who were the sources for the rest of this? bartenders and barbouncers and disco DJs, an incompetent candidate for a regional legislature, the owner of a settlement's only electronics outlet where Yury had bought brake fluid and nine volt batteries once, and, of course, obviously, local girls—girls who'd declined advances, girls with kasha teeth and bellies like pregnant dumplings who swore they'd refused 'the friend', who promised they hadn't been refused *by him*——never a girl eventually filmed, never One who'd become a star).

Usually the morning after they'd met at whichever hamlet's lone bar or wannabe club he'd call her whose number he'd tattooed dramatically along an arm in the midst of frenzied dancing——he'd call early to disorient, waking the girl only to do her the favour of giving her an hour, for her parents to clear out for work, for her to apply razor, makeup, brush (he and Yury slept in the van or, if awake, 'the friend' would flip through last night's polaroids).

They'd arrange an interview as if *this was* a professional engagement——this was a professional engagement——meeting for creamed coffees at the hamlet's sole barclub reopened by morning as a canteen serving what can now be confirmed as a light but succulent Fruhstuck (when 'the friend' wanted to persuade through intelligence he'd find the German word).

There he might ask straight out to see some identification. The other conceit was inducement: he might neg and argue and feign incredulity, convincing the girl it was her idea to show it to him——figuring if she'd spread her wallet, she'd spread something else.

It was only when he saw her sum that he solicited (with allowances, reportedly, for girls whose age of consent was within a year or two or three).

After this vetting the appointment might adjourn to the van, its wheels astride the canteen's curb, where Yury, bleary, would buckle the girl up front and interpret the terms on the dash——explaining, or obscuring, the particulars involved, then guiding her hand to fondle the appropriate releases ('This is a translated contract, it says the same as it does in English,' except it doesn't).

Though obviously an encounter like this was no guarantee, especially not when compared to an email——the prospects who'd responded to the ad, the pursued pursuing, seeking stigma with alingual typos.

That ad, being untranslated, flattered:

It said, If you can understand this you're special and deserve to be treated specially, you're the elect, lucky enough to give us an address and we'll drive up direct, hump our grip up eighteen flights of stairs to knock on your door (the elevators having been installed out of order)——you'll open and greet us, you'll hug us and kiss us, you've won us, we'll ply you with substance in thanks, then strip and fuck you for posterity——with your husbands and fathers and boyfriends out belabouring the docks and hangars, ensconced behind their paleotechnic computer terminals the size of motelrooms, slobby in their pinching jeans and unironic tshirts, too tired to prevent or remedy.

You don't have to leave your tower, which was an identical copy of the prior tower visited, you don't have to leave your apartment, which was a perfect clone of the previous 'flat'—a number of the females surveyed spoke a studious Anglo-English—you don't even have to be sober, shouldn't have to be sober again (the substances provided were vodochka, a nailbite of cocaine). If porn was concrete, these girls were cement—cement being the most important component of concrete, what makes concrete stick, what makes it bind, the rest is just sand, water, and air—without these girls, the porn would never adhere, the screens would go blank, the towers would crumble.

In winter, on a junket to a smaller burg whose snow and ice kept the populace indoors, 'the friend' proposed to meet a girl vanside, parking that bloodbright mobile in the square by the townhall and plague column, by the manger and tree, by the monuments to horsebacked wars saddling generations with occupation. He drove the girl to her dacha—which was abandoned for the season—where they dressed a tripod in her clothes for a scarecrow, put a picnic blanket down and thawed the garden.

Another winter another dacha, but this dacha used yearround since the family had been evicted from their permanent residence for nonpayment. The girl's deaf or blind or both deaf and blind grandmother was exiled to the kitchen, while Mama—laid off from her banktelling shift, home from selling knitwear in the market—joined in her horny self—no need to look at *her ID*.

However, all prospectives were made aware: if there were ever any parental or supervisory issues that rendered filming in their cinderblock villa or cottage not feasible, or just undesirable, 'the friend' was prepared to relocate to virtually any area cemetery, junkyard, or gully and fuck in the back bay of the sanguineous van—amid the hubby spare tires and jutting jack the encompassing external drives and menagerie of woofers and tweeters—with always newly purchased, still in its shrink plastic bedding rolled down: latex beneath her, latex inside.

They'd make do with the van instead of renting a room or putting up at a pension—but was this because the accommodations available were so horrible (the bedbugs scuffling, hatched from the sconces)? or because when a room was cheap, its trouble was free? As policy, shakedown money, to neighbourhood operators or the mafiavory, never was paid. Yury kept a gun in his pants, the uncircumcised coming more naturally than feminine circumspection. This amateurishness, a voluble amateurishness, was their aesthetic, all of theirs.

And finally—after the rubber was removed to unleash another manner of voluble across a girl's eyebrows—there'd be an outro Q & A, postmortem.

How much did you like it?

I liked it *moc!* very much!

Last session, 'the friend' had mislaid the cards, and a vibrating pouch of dildos

F

and lube, and so here he'd had to improvise—with bottoms ripped from pizzaboxes scrawled across with marker:

'My name is YOUR NAME. Today I had my first sex on camera.'

Say it, he said, waving the cardboard spotted with cheesegobs and grease.

My name is YOUR NAME, today I—but this peroxidised little sister of a girl he'd had the previous Easter was interrupted by a drip in her eye.

Just for you @, 'the friend' prompted, and the sister, who'd been sororally recommended, repeated.

Say, Goodbye.

That day might have seen this girl's first sex on camera, but not on film—nobody used film. Rather they used a format more indestructible, yet even more evanescent—Digital. 'The friend's' digit dangled at its largest size, glabrousized. Then shrank at sixty frames per second.

After the redlight was no light, was dead light, it was his turn in the shower. He towelled his cock dry, put it to sleep in the cinch of a drawstring.

Yury was packed.

By the time our peroxider had gathered her halter and mini and arose—she'd ascended—upon her pleather stilettos, 'the friend' had seeped through his pants.

So was she still named *Natasha?* or was she *Molly* [from] *Darabani*, as she was posted last week? or was she *Poly* [sic] *Sofia*, as the commentariat corrected? but what about this

Obsessa O'dessa—is it me, or did I take ballet class with her?

Anyway, her name was never *Natasha*—she'd given 'the friend' the name of a friend.

In their vignette, 'the friend' called himself *Greg.*

Now *Natasha* did it for the rush, *Molly* out of desperation, and Poly liked the cash—but what about the girl who bore them all, gravid with their shame?

She did it for the hope.

These women lived in hope, they lived for the future as if they were every one of them already characters in a movie that projected well beyond one orgasm's duration—a movie of constant orgasm being constantly filmed: a wishful collectivist biopic accumulating footage—incessantly accumulating reels and gigabytes of footage—for all that dirty work of editing into coherence and happy endings somewhere years from now and countries away.

They lived as the aspiring stars of the movies of their own lives, which themselves contained the movies of others (much as nuclear reactors contain their cores):

Like the Innocent boy from around the block movie about an Innocent boy from around the block who begins driving a better sportscar and sporting better muscles, crucified in a black leather jacket, hung with gold chains (though he sold heroin substitute, though it was said he sold women—look how motivated he is, look how rich—*Innokenti, I remember when we both were just kids*).

Like the movie about the defence contractor billionaire who'd financed a production of his own out in northeastern Randomstan, but without even filming it, with epic thousands of extras but no cameras or crew: it'd been a Passion play, one night only staged on the steppe, ever since being nearly hazed to death as an Air Force mechanic he'd wanted to experience that many people taking orders from him—the one about the former bricklayer turned gas refinery tycoon who, to repent for having inflicted Orthodox baptism on his 10 year old stepdaughter (and to mortar his relationship with her mother, a lingerie importer), had bought the girl her own television broadcast: she'd babble to the world about her friends, boys, school, and sport for an hour each night at eleven—the port concessions magnate who'd financed a judge's vanity recording of Liszt—the financial services mogul who'd commissioned a mural of his transgender mistress/master for a flank of his bank—the politician who'd hired a Muscovite screenwriter to ghostwrite a book exposing the corruption of his, the screenwriter's, uncle, a Navy embezzler who'd sunk submarines: the nephew took the work, he was broke.

This was an ambitious time and the girls knew their movies—they knew those had by hearsay or passed down the bulvar as well as they knew those of their siblings and intimates—they traded their stakes and plot points and narrative arcs—they quoted from them until they couldn't separate the quotes from their own conversation—they repeated and repeated them, you couldn't avoid them, you can't avoid summary—they even ambitiously invented them to reinvent themselves:

A man thrashed his wife whose head spurted oil—another billion, trillion—googillionaire. A man from the next town over, it was said, always just the next town, battered the gut of his pregnant wife and their son was born fluent in C++ and Chinese. Soon he had women at his door lining three deep, begging him to go to work on their issue. Then yet another nouveau oligarch who'd kickstarted his fortune marketing fire extinguishers throughout the Baltics or Balkans, parlaying that lode into funding lucrative ecommerce interests—it was said (apparently, it even made international headlines), he intended to launch a blue whale into space and was designing a shuttle whose fuselage would be equipped with a seawater tank. Once safely in orbit, the tank's hatch would open, releasing the water and whale to float dead forever in blackness—our earth a bruise the size of its eye. . . .

But the most successful of these movies, the widest cited, it seemed—whenever a teacher assigned the composition theme of *Hope*, whenever any of the girls skipped their composition tutorials to hitchhike to the gorge for a swim only because they were young with plombir skin and fit and ruthless and happened to spot speeding from the opposite cardinality a vehicle as red as (some of these epithets were used, others are fictitious) 'the Soviet flag', 'a fire siren', 'the covers of the Russian passport', 'menarche'—was this, was the story of 'Mary Mor'.

Which is also the story of the unpopular Hollywood film SLEEPWAKER V, dir. Edison Lips, 1998.

SLEEPWAKER V is the most famous but also only film of this 'Mary Mor,' who does not star in it with her name shining pointedly above the title, but plays Hotty #3, whose total screentime is $\leq$ forty-five seconds.

'Hotty Mor' as she was called—with the accents of these tellings a binomial classification perhaps best transliterated as *Chotty Mor* or *Khoti Mor*—was a success story to trump all success stories, her movie widely heard of but seldom seen—it became more potent the longer it went unviewed, as if an ineffable dictator.

She was a model of what every girl wanted—not just an actress, was she a model too?

Her recent naturalisation by the United States government revealed her to be Toyta Dzhakhmadkalova—and this attempted journalism, this inept investigative reporting, is dedicated to her.

She was born atop a tiny speck of static blown just outside Vedeno, Vedensky District, Chechnya, a mudspot like a mortifying stain on the dress of the land. Must be laundered, must be treadwashed by tanks. Russian was not her native language, she had no dialogue, she was frequently silent. Her home, an apartment complex hastily built to gird Vedeno's outskirts, has been almost totally destroyed. It was, by the time of her leaving, that proverbial heap of concrete surrounded by field the colour of a suicidebombed circus and the miry consistency of mad tigress dung. The following things, things being weaknesses, made her cry: faded wallpaper in a scythe pattern similar to what they had in the kitchen of her family's apartment (but every family had similar wallpaper), last cigarettes not shared, dying ficus placed by unsunned windows (in apartments where none of the windows were sunned), cold tea—and now, for the uninitiated, the briefest of history lessons: border skirmishes by separatist guerillas vs. Russians, Russian army incursions, hilariously vituperative decades of on again off again conflict you might've caught on television or not.

It has not been recorded—how Toyta found her way to Grozny (lit. *terrible*), capital of the Chechen Republic, following the First Chechen War. Perhaps she was there visiting a relative close or distant, the aunt of her aunt she called aunt too, the wife of a father's friend from hydroelectric engineering school she called Peacock—because of the woman's plumage, the feather she tied to her braid—but privately. Supposed to meet her at the bus terminal. Never knew which three o'clock train. Nor is it known how Toyta was supposed to have supported herself. Whether she cooked for monks or did laundry for a nearby madrassa, whether she cleaned floors for whatever government offices were left or washed windows in what official residences in the diplomatic quarter hadn't been razed. What retails as fact is that one night in an impromptu Grozny discotheque (formerly a dairy) she met a Russian soldier——cleancut, tightbodied, tightclothed in uniform plus mufti sneakers——who managed through bribing a general it must have been to bring her back to the site of his patriarchate: 180 kilometres outside Moscow and then, for a weekend, to Moscow Herself, neighbourhood Ostankino, where a comrade soldier also discharged had an uncle who commanded a balcony over Zvyozdny (but the uncle spent whole months what was characterised as consulting in Crimea).

We will pause here to allow you to recite your PIN numbers to yourself.

By Saturday Night 1996, she'd escaped a Ciscaucasian death. Toyta would become, if the girls who'd tell this story were aware of the concept, *Immortal*——which Slavic languages too tend to render in the negative, as if it were regrettable: 'never-dying', 'never-ending'. At a bar in Moscow she left her soldier for a visiting American, a roving producer of pornographic movies.

This reporter was told that though the bar's ambiance blarneyed Irish, its name was very much of its place and time, ambitious, nearly excessively utopian: The Brothel Under the Sign of the Dice with Three Faces, Where Lesbians Drink Free on Sundays, Male Homosexuals Eat Free Every Second Monday, Where Behind One of the Toilet Tanks Is Said to be Hidden a Jew's Treasure and the Rook's Nest in the Garderobe Has Been Formed from the World's Longest Lime Twig That if Ever Unravelled into Its Original Curvature Would Spell Out the Word *Typewriter* . . . (but I think here I might've been toyed with).

You ask, you might, how could an American who respects women and gives them jobs with equal wages and higher ed degrees and diligently keeps his paws off them——how could he ever expect with his solicitousness and always asking and nerves to take a woman away from a Russian soldier? from an officer——we've just promoted him——an officer with holstered sidearm, this major in Czarish bluegreens the colour of a Romanov's blood? To answer that, however, you'd have to think bigger than masculinity, bigger than the sexpower of violence, of war. It should be understood that the American in the sideways porkpie hat still dangling its pricetag was no mere gap year visitor or sex tourist but an approximate Russian himself (such is the nature of the American problem: who are you? whose are you?), an émigré who'd come to the United States in 1984 or thereabouts via Israel and was here returned to Moscow——though he was born in St. Petersburg, or Leningrad, and had never been to Moscow before——recruiting talent or the eligibly cheap.

After Toyta had filmed a luxuriously uxorious——read: unremunerated——scene in his room in the starriest hotel in Moscow (don't believe it but this is what he almost certainly had her believe: with marble baths, marble sinks, marble floors, with beds as rare and expensive as arabescato and just as uncomfortable to stay the night in), this hyphenated-American, this Russian–Israeli–Floridian——Iosif, Yossele, let's call him Joe, regular Joe——procured for her a legitimate work visa #HıB and flew her to Los Angeles, whose airport bears the acronym LAX.

Los Angeles, despite belonging to dreams, also belongs to America. This means that Toyta's life was set, her survival assured by Marines. Here she could become someone named Tanya and this Tanya Someone could become a success. The rest, the denouement as it's said in film, the finale, is scarcely as important.

In LA, Toyta/Tanya became Tina Toy, then, because she was once mercilessly lashed with the word 'tiny' by a wheelchaired dominatrix in a Thai noodlerie's ladies' room, 'your waist is soooo tiny!'——Tanya/Tina at the mirror slurping up the word in an endlessly looping waist of *tiny tiny tiny*——she became Tiny Toy, until a reputable casting agent she met at an audition for a low budget, character driven thriller told her she'd had her typed from name alone as black, not white and foreign——and so she became Mary Moor, who became Mary Mor (both at the suggestion of a Brit cameraman with bum knees who'd tried to date her), because in porn, which genre it seemed she'd be condemned to forever, there was already an established Mary More, another tanned to public transport upholstery texture girl with platinised tresses once notorious for the development of her kegels but now on her way out who, due to unspecified viruses——definitely herpes, allegedly hepatitides——could perform by industry decree only when protected, with the man maintaining on his erection a condom.

Toyta, for her part, was never infected with the worst of the diseases you could contract in America——doubt——she was positively immune to fear and doubt and so was incapable of being anything but fun, firm, and objectively reckless (not even that monthly test could scare her: the butch boss nurse, the kit's prick, a fink of blood to clog the vial——while waiting, she counted, the results always arriving punctually, by thirty).

It was on the set of a pornographic movie whose title has not survived and whose content has since like a failed family been broken up into short few minute clips all over the internet and there, meaning everywhere, aggregated under myriad descriptors and tags (the disparate keywords: *Teen——Interracial, Anal, Trib, POV, Mary Mor*), that she met a porno actor who——due to his 12" fame, the presumed prowess that went along with it, along with a concomitant legend regarding the size of the loads he routinely 'unloaded'——was asked to play weekly poker with legitimate Hollywood television and film actors who only minced and otherwise faked the act of sex for much more money than was paid the people, just as attractive, who had sex really.

One Sunday during a game of Texas hold 'em, he ('Neo' of the prickly cactus muscles and tribal tatts, his head to toe entirely depilated) raved to his host's brother inlaw—this producer/director Edison—about his costar Mary—super*bott*—recommending her as a miscellaneous Eastern girl / stripper / prostitutka who might even be able to negotiate small speaking roles, ten words or less, tiny.

A boa slithered down a chairback. Edison's inlaw, an awardwinning screenwriter with an intellectual reputation, entirely intolerant of the career of his wife's kitschmacher brother, weekly invited the owner of a prominent Animal Handling company to play because the man, who worked only for topflight productions—dogs only for the best children's dogmovies, his lizards and apes regularly preferred over computer effects no matter how perfected—brought the snakes. A month before, and he could've lost his license for this, he'd brought a baby lion. 'Leo' prowled around the balmy house, was soon forgotten and lost, only later did they find it stuck in the dryer.

The Animal Handler said this Sunday:

Them women from over there are gorgeous. But I don't know they're worth the trouble.

He proceeded to tell the story of a friend and onetime employee (a janitor, a hoser) who had, he said, Ordered one of them from one of them services online—they sent her off and she ruined him, took every fucking follicle.

(The boa was coiled safely in a donut box.)

No fault divorce, he said, no shit, wasn't no time for fault. Four years in this country and the cunt was entitled to half.

Edison, shockhaired, sensitively chinned—before he produced he'd inherited his father's storage facilities throughout LA, he'd joke on first dates that he'd inherited *emptiness*—told Neo to tell Toyta to come by the studio next Friday and—Hotty #3 was born. A minuscule part, a negligible role (Neo's bluff was called by a rash of queens, he'd left down 2K to Edison).

The film was the fifth in a series, a franchise—the fifth sequel, the pentaquel perhaps—but who recalled what the first four had been about, what'd happened in them when and where, who'd lived or died while making adolescent love on a rope bridge restive above a torrid ravine in Ventura steep enough to roll the credits down, there was no sense before there was no continuity. . . .

. . . The old man, lupine, spry, and hairy, wiped down the bar and continued his story:

Unfortunately our Hotty's only line was cut, for being unintelligible. A tragedy —her words.

He paused, drank some sort of murky plumwater, took puffs on a short handrolled stub.

But then somebody uploaded that scene to the internet, he said, where to this day you can find it.

F

He turned behind the bar to wind the clock.

Business was changing, he said.

Movies where you sat in the dark with a hundred people groping one another gave way to television where you sat in the dark by yourself. Then the internet came around, cords became cordless, wires became wireless, suddenly entertainment was free and everyone's an amateur—amateurs at being themselves—because only celebrities are lucky enough to get paid just for being. Buy a camera, convince your bestlooking kinsfolk, upload, and Play—no more packaging, no more distribution where the smut's hauled out to the far bazaars among the bahns. This was democracy, this was enfranchisement, all that other sluttery you sold us—CocafuckingCola, shiny motorcycles parked between the legs of our mothers.

The bartender's eyes were elder, rheumy, his mouth disfigured, raggedly burnt and rimmed with moles like acastellated ashtray, like the hoops and arches of a crown. He snuffed his rollie, cleared the ashtray behind the bar.

His nose was a sharply tuned muzzle, was a hatchet. He was wolfish, vicious.

He said, Toyta returned to doing porn after her serious stint—she was savvy. She founded her own singlefee, multipass network—a dozen sites, a dozen girls, independents under her personal curation. An entrepreneura—that and not any implanted measurements is why her story is still told.

(I'm certainly polishing his English. Through the flit of whiskers he was facile but incorrect and interspersed locutions in French, in German, Italian—I've also filled in details and—no, you'll decide.)

It's said that the neighbour of her Grozny aunt had a daughter who was sold via Ukrainians to an au pairship in the West. My own—*Grossnichte*, *Grossnichte*—grandnieces, yes, grandnieces ended as Gulf commodities, whored to the oily emirates, the sheikh sex dens of Dubai—

F

X   X   X

HE——I——SAT LISTENING TO THIS STORY, to the script of this tale and to others. Dizzied by the dates and locales, the vertiginous names——what lingua!

He sat on a stool at the bar and let this wizened bartender give him an education——this tender who'd taught himself the idiom by studying a UK travelguide 'to Swiss'. He had a cigarette and a drink, unidentifiable, he was learning how to smoke and how to drink, he'd been abroad for a month already but was not going back, he felt as if he'd graduated from even himself, that he was a new person now waiting only to receive the new skin to prove it——signed by no one, signifying nothing.

In the vid, behind Moc's head, a calendar had hung. The image on the page for the month of May showed a bouquet of blossoming trees——birch?/dogwood?/willow?——in front of the castle he'd stood in front of that morning (apparently, it was a renowned castle, though arduous to find——tired afterward he'd wandered into this bar at random, it had about it the rogue air of foreignness, of youth).

He'd had reprinted——at a kiosk in a webcafe huddled between a shashlik stand and a kvassarium——a stack of that screengrab, which froze mild May above Moc chastely clothed, or in that interim declothing phase (it was the only frame that satisfied all criteria): just her face and, regrettably, perhaps the top cleave of her breasts. He'd been asking around for weeks: Is this setting in any way familiar? do you recognise the girl or just last month? He'd handed one to this proprietor's hispid paw not an hour before——this proprietor who called himself Publicov and was closer to being an upright verbose lupus than anything human.

How do I know you're not another filmmaker? Publicov asked. Or maybe this Moc owes you money and you want to do worse things to her than what is done for the pleasuring of cameras?

He said to Publicov, You have to believe me——I was sent by her family in America.

Now she has family in America? The barwolf sucked his lips, fanged stiff the hair around them.

Cousins——I'm Moc's cousin from Jersey.

Roland Jersey——what did you say you were called?

Orlando, he said, Orlando Kirsch (first name the city his mother was born in, last name that of his father's orthodontist).

Publicov said, I don't know what I'm looking at, and lit another rollie.

F

Izvinitye, turning away from the smoke to busy with the bottles——containments un-
dusted, displayed like women tall and smooth and without protuberance, ranks of
uncomplicated women, easier to uncork, easier to pour.

But Publicov hadn't returned the printout, it lay like a rag sopping up the bar——the
same printout posted that morning all over the ornate ironwork gates surrounding the
calendared castle, on grave crucifixes in the dim midden yards of ruined churches,
across the graffitied walls of gnomish humpy bunkers and imperious towers——glued
and taped and stickered and tacked and nailed.

He asked Publicov, Please keep an eye out for her, telling him he was staying at
a certain 'Hotel Romantical', where he'd also left the desk clerk, an obliging pink boy
of approximately his age, with a sheaf.

There was no text on this primitive poster save an address for an email account
he'd opened the night of his arrival: meetingmoc@moc.com—— the new address of his
newest domain, $5/month in perpetuity it cost, and his bank, his parents' account at the
bank, was scheduled to make the payment on the first of the month, the first of every
month, and to do so indefinitely or until his parents' funds were depleted, which meant
this empty website——*We're Under Construction, We're Still Under Construction*——and
its full inbox of tipsters' emails might outlive him.

Publicov, finished prepping for lunch's rush, turned to him and said as if in
afterthought, And you might not want to try asking the police.

He said, So I won't.

We'll drink to that, and Publicov poured himself a glass, then refilled his, both to
their brims. Together they clinked, took down the warm shots coloured like a bruise.
Publicov's glass hit a tooth, a slimy cuspid, which fell out and soaked in the dregs, a
lonely rottenfaced fang. The bar was beginning to fill with customers, with noon, and
Publicov must have been distracted. The drink tasted like the colours of the walls, like
the turpentine that would remove that black. That spore, accreted grime.

The windows were open, the door, like a wing, aflutter. The crowd, on
surrounding stools, in chairs at wheeltop tables, was vocal, was warming——they
were sweating what they had drunk. Bluish ghosts wisped from their lungs but above
him hovered only a miniature white cloud and he did not suspect his cigarette brand,
he suspected himself, his soul (and hungered for a waitress——he wondered why there
wasn't one around).

In a high nook, nested amid a thatching of cables, a television was playing
sport——which sport he didn't recognise, he was too impaired. It wasn't darts——because
that was being played against the door with a kitchen knife——nor was it a game
exclusively of running or jumping. The rules, assuming there were any, involved a
ball round like a spot but spotted itself, impregnated with a rambunctious demon, it
hopped and skipped and jumped around as a team of perhaps fifty grown men had to

F

run and avoid it, because it wanted to hit them and kill them, and the men could run but they could run only in the confines of the stadium, and the stadium, as the volume was lowered throughout the afternoon, got smaller and quieter until it was just a silent spit of light and he was alone with Publicov, who handed him his bill.

Dusk was just beginning, in the bar it was almost too dark to read—anyway the napkin had too many numbers.

He might have been drunk but still hadn't imbibed that much and said so and Publicov, offended, said, But it is only an address, maybe it will help.

Thank you, Publicov.

He thought, this book—this will be a book—is hereby respectfully dedicated to you.

He walked through the dusk to clear the head, to sober. Give himself time to decide whether to walk or be taken by what'd take him. The wind blew harshly, exhaled from the debauched cherubs' cheeks of the arcades. Lampposts lofted lamps that were out but the posts themselves were justification enough, drastic lancing efflorescences, metal trees set starkly against the greyscale of the sky. He decided on a taxi but couldn't find a taxi, could find no tram either, no tramstop though there were tracks over which to stumble, no buses or huffy marshrutky despite the poles that served as stops where he'd plastered over the timetables with posters of his Moc. Each cobble felt like a hill he had to ascend, a mountain, between them deep smutted river valleys filled with 50ml nipbottles filled with the messages of wet butts. Pedestrians, mere bundles of cloths and threads and yarns, baskets with pasty arms and legs protruding and, from the tops, heads swollen like kerchiefed treats, passed him in the street, their very lives averted. Setts and pavingblocks gave way to a prospekt expansive enough for the parade of tanks and trucks in convoy, pulsing traffic away from the asbestine heart installed at the horizon—this city's entire historical centrum, intended only for the necrophiles and thanatos tourists, giving way to asphalt, the fancy fachwerk and gingerbread façades faded, even that fairy castle smogged, the leanings of centuries collapsed into piles of wood and stone until only boxes remained.

As if cardboard boxes, crates for the packing, stacked into towers, these hundreds or thousands of modular units making of the suburbs a boundless concatervation—as if the world had surrendered its rolling fields and city streets and instead cast itself up, straight up, as if the three dimensions of our experience had been upended, to two—as if he were headed toward not an address but a setting, a set . . .

How to explain such a scene to Sunday brunch readers at home? How to situate you—how to acquaint you but only with words?

Your correspondent did not know, your apprentice artist had not an inkle, how to describe the towering above him. Think not of livingspace, of cosy homes in distant faubourgs and kieze, but of officeparks, think of malls. Risen tiers and superseding

F

levels of commerce, of store. But not stores as you might be used to them.

Where offices and shops should have been were domiciles, were private apartments—though from the outside, approaching the pathwork from the windblown street, they provided anything but privacy. They were glassed, they were entirely glassed floor to ceiling and any visitor could see in. He could look in where an accountancy should be and there was a family arguing at supper. Observe where managers should reign and surveil a grandfather at stool. Hello, grandfather! How are you feeling? how commoted are your bowels this evening?

A building cubicled, celled, seen—its exterior lit from within into a screen. The lobby door was locked, a smashed metal door loosely locked. He twisted the knob and pulled, pulled. He checked the address again and the address was correct, unless a disgruntled resident had reaudited some numerals. Someone would leave, he was certain, he didn't know why he was certain—so vitrined, everyone appeared exhausted, appeared asleep.

He waited but no one came. He leaned against the jamb and, though he didn't know which unit he was looking for, tempted the buzzers, which were anyway unlabelled. He buzzed one and then another and yet another, but they were not buzzers. They didn't buzz an apartment with a familiar tone so that the party buzzed would be alerted that he was outside downstairs waiting for the door to open—instead they were eavesdroppers, they were monitors. When he pressed one he heard, through the fixture's grill, a baby's tin crying, when he pushed a second he overheard gerocomically gluttonous breath, fingering still a third, it was ragged sex, while from others was speakered indistinct talking, murmuration and scold, snoring, a lot of snoring and even silence, but needless to say only the silence baffled—perhaps that apartment was vacant or its buzzer, broken—and he didn't comprehend any conversation.

Moc—if she was in residence—which foursquare screen above him was her gleaming? which button would give him access to her sighs? In his hand, Publicov's napkin was streaking, had smirched—never having noted which floor was hers, it was presently expressive of even less: just a clot of phlegm, a florid spew. He considered hurling it like a rock at a pane—then went scrounging for a more stolid embodiment under a precise hedgerow welded to the ground—but there were no rocks and there was a redundance of panes. He threw the paper and away it flew. The swingset had no swings. The slide was a ladder up. The weather was as oppressively changeless as the consecution of the development's paths.

The door clicked and out staggered a group of intimidating children, overgrown children. Their youths were stuffed like sausages into the casings of overalls, in the fashion of gastarbeiters, their faces were slabs of borodinbread swabbed with butter, their noses whole potatoes and ears, the toothpicked rinds, their fingers livid burns as from carelessness with methpipes. They stared at him, spoke cacophonic codes and then——nudging one of their race forward, a manboy with crusty, distended lips, trollishly stunted——inquisitioned:

Does David ever make it back home——or, *Ever go home do David?* or, *Did home ever David make go?* and though through the measured, mechanical accent he understood the words because they were in his language, he didn't know what they meant until, a breath, he realised they referred not to him, rather to an American television show he'd never watched but had heard of——a hysterical serial, he thought, impossible not to have heard of (though it'd been over for a season, its antics supplanted), as he told this insistent, scarcarved, tough as warts horde:

Yes, David goes back home to marry Samara from college——though his father dies or is kidnapped for ransom, but only after his mother's investment firm fails or is arsoned, I hesitate to say which, and no——he said in answer to the youngest trollnik stroking his leg——no, I don't know what happened to your sister!

They lured him into the tower talking as if talk would be enough to resist them——them grasping at every scrap, at jeanpocket and jacketflap, at the frayed bills filched from his pockets and at coins——down a hallway suffused with noxious stench: fuming nettles, as if in the production of a remedy for this hallucination in progress.

The back of the tower was not, like its frontage, glassed, but concrete poured floors above a courtyard. Only the front's sheer veneer was new.

It was a courtyard strung across with links for laundry——light frilly cirri of negligee and peignoir, lowhanging nimbi of thong and garter——filled with receptacles and trash. And he was tossed like a bag of trash himself——thrown atop the bags, rolled over their blackly bodied putrescence, needle shards of mirror, a slough of diapered spoiled lard——tumbling into another hall, to his knees at the threshold of an opposite tower.

The boys emerged from behind——having slipped past the dumpsters at the yard's periphery——dragged him to his feet, to an entryway as dark as fur.

Just inside, seated in a chair with a singular daintiness, was a bear. A bear distinctly untaxidermical. It was a crossdressing bear, if animals can be said to be transvestite, if creatures have enough gender identity to make their wearing of the opposite sex's human clothing something approaching a meaningful statement, any statement at all. A pince-nezed male shebear in a windsocklooking bonnet speckled with sunflowers, above skirts of billowing hospitalgowns patched with flag, the vex of a nation he could not place. The entirety had been cashiered from a fable, discharged from a land of porridgecomplexioned dwarves (his youthful escort, assembling protectively around).

The mamabear gestured him to a chair of his own, of a similar make: a fussy interiorism high of haunch, tiny of limb——as if not a perch but perched itself, upon fluted legs, the feet with chiselled toenails, with claws——upholstered in pelage, in uncomfortable quills that rustled with every shift and he shifted, he couldn't force himself to keep still. Between the chairs was a table as swarmed as the sexagenary square of a chessboard, draped with a drab spiderweb lace doily, set with a corroded samovar fixtured with a bulb, its stray filament illuminating two saucers, two companion cups. A battered phrasebook's pages folded down. Not a phrasebook but his passport, atop his wallet, blueblack both. And the keys to a faraway home tenanted, it must've been, by faraway and worried parents.

It was the dusty sittingroom of a pensioner with no children or none who visited regularly, only the relict thievelets who, kissing their mamabear's jewelled paw, raised that dust in the rowdy muster of departure. They shut the door behind them—that door set flush with the shadows—spun its lock, as if adjusting a radio, or as a vault is sealed—suddenly, it was as if he wasn't sitting in a room anymore but amid night itself.

He felt tickling, below it all—but how had he not noticed—a rug of bearskin.

His host growled in response to this inspection, said, Publicov's no liar—he said he'd never met anyone who wants a girl like you do.

So what type do you want, my dear? of what species, my dearest? I have every model in stock.

Slav slave or Central Asian combination? vagina where the anus is or anus where the vagina is? there's nothing we don't do: oral exclusive, mutual masturbation, S&M, gruppengrope, frottage.

I want one, he said, her name is Moc.

Roleplay then?

No role, Moc.

No doubt we have her too—with this, the bear madame growled a woman from out of the fuscation: a big brutish wench with a figure like a log her employer could hibernate inside, who looped her wildweed hair and pouted lechy her smacked black lip, where she had a sore.

That's not her.

Of course it's her—the newest version. You won't recognise the difference.

I want Moc.

You would.

The woman's giant trunking mass dulled abruptly into furniment again: secretaire, escritoire—into nothing that refined, just a handleless lunk of domesticated linden. Where you'd keep a will you'd like to lose.

And I want immortality, said Madame bear, but I can't have it—I want to own a helicopter and a yacht and a gym franchise, I want to downsize half my staff and fix the lottery in Kyiv—but who can live from wishes?

Who?

F

Having held every other bodypart, his hands could hold his hands.

Madame bear sniffed, said, OK, so you're searching for this Moc——I'll tell you what, I'll help you, I'll tell you how to find Her.

And from now on, dearest Reader, it's too late to doubt——

There is, the bear said, a place.

Then it covered itself with a shawl, tugged from a puddle in its lap——the fringe of that rug of bearskin, omnivorously soiled, full of thistle.

It was deeper night and eurous gusts found the spaces between words to fill them with their chill.

This isn't a story, David, *this is a place* (and here another creature's prose is indiscriminately enhanced: the bear's original locutions being even more melodramatic, more foreboding, stalled by tedious epistolaries)——but it is Far far away, it is dangerously enchanted.

The bear paused to siphon tea for two from the samovar looming like a fervid moon above them. Lighting his wallet, lighting his keys.

The brew was black and ropy, with a hint of citrus, of bergamot, then, he sipped again——it was still too hot——this taste unplaced, hot and dull but rublesucking sour.

He put his cup back on the saucer, placed the saucer atop his passport for a coaster: his passport picture, he felt, already out of date——it was mortifying and he hoped the bear wouldn't ask to examine it, wouldn't comment.

Or it both exists and doesn't exist, the bear went on, I myself don't know how it manages that, but you will.

My lovely, my darling.

Though when you'd know is precisely when you'd no longer be able to tell me

It's distant, David, I can tell you that, then once there, go higher.

Go high atop a mountain, a hill that's been fortified, a walled settlement walled deep in the past.

At least you'd think it was centuries ago——all that mud, that woodstirred mud. Before electricity even——this is important——before all that current that connects the world like lines of latitude, reception like lines of longitude, the equator of constant signal.

The houses look that old too, they look ancient, they're falling down, their foundations rotted stumps, sinking, sunk, their roofs are thatched and leaking weather.

There in the centre of town, because it is a town, there in the centre of the centre as if the hub where all the wheelspokes meet, is a square, and in the centre of that square is a well and if you gaze and gaze and gaze into that well late at midnight you will see, it's said, your own reflection——this is because there's a measure of water at the bottom——what else would you expect to see down there, tell me?

F

But.

(The bear tugged tight its holeworn shawl—that thorny fluff indistinguishable from its fur—then crossed one leg over another like a popular child psychologist, and this struck him as faintly ridiculous: one claw resting on a claw of the chair—the bear was smaller than he'd thought, it didn't reach the floor.)

But the inhabitants of this town—they are why it's so special, David, Orlando, friendly Greg—whatever you wish to be called.

Cinching its socky bonnet, the bear's ears skewed out the sides: mangled ears, one lively, the other limp, like the rushing minute and lagged hour hands of a clock.

When a girl like Moc decides to shed her coy lycras and molt her cloying denims to engage in sexual intercourse on camera, that's when it happens—that's when the, shall we say, 'funniness' happens.

(Please forgive my language—when you recall in your own words how I've told this tale to you tonight I hope you'll have me speaking better.)

This is a special change I refer to, a sort of conversion. After they're shot, if you'll follow my explanation, after these girls are shot, they cease to exist.

Rather I'm speaking of an existence that's not an existence—after these girls are filmed doing what it is they do, they no longer belong to themselves but to the world, as they're no longer merely physical but image too, they are everywhere, they are everyone's.

Where do they exist then, ask yourself, *if they do?*

In themselves, in their own skin, or as imagined—as unimagined—on the screen in your lap?

They become women/nonwomen—having been used, having been overused, and so weakened, weak, there's a grain and a haze to them, a sapping depletion (indeed, everyone's fate is the same and is sordid).

Not anymore pure people of skeletonised flesh, yet also not purely data transmission of image and sound, they dwell instead in the middle—limboed, in an interim stage—abiding a gaplife as something between.

At best as an essence of what they once were—half theirs and half yours now: David's, Orlando's, gregarious Gregory and Yury's—shut into this secret repository, into this archive they live in, a cache of the senselessly undead.

For steadiness he sipped at his now tepid bitter tea, keeping his eyes on the rude snout of his ursal host, on the ear that kept twitchily ticking.

Your Moc—the bear producing a rumpelskin paper from a slit in its parachute housedress, the printout showing the Missing caged on a page, caged in a screen, depicting the Wanted at the very beginning of mid-act—your Moc is not as she was, but she is still herself.

She has already entered that other realm, that porousness beyond borders, that

F

Freedom. . . .

The bear crumpled a corner of the printout in its paw, dipped it in its own tea (untouched), began eating it wet. Those eyes nailing themselves into his. As drops of the drink smeared its fur, matting the fur that was just then wrapping around him, he who couldn't help but stare——at that lewd dewy snout, that lurid ear tick, the sharpened nails of those eyes——couldn't help but close his own now, he was exhausted, he was softly enfolded, he apologised, mumbling, he hadn't properly slept in over a month. . . .

X X X

(notes for a videographer)

HE WAKES IN THE FOREST. It is dark and it is thick, with green and brown like the swirl of a clogged toilet. Wastepaper hanging from the trees, lots of trees. Sweaty profferings of verd as if not grown but enlusted, bouquets of let loose bush. Pubescent stalks sprung up between pawprints, deep but shallowly filled, like wells with toes, with talons, their moisture stagnant, a dankness pervades, the stalks decompose. Evidence of uprootings. Trees big and wet——when did it rain? up on their roots exposed like rusted struts, like scaffold. Hills just ahead like steppingstones to hills, like stones topped with walls of trees, with a sky of trees screening out the sun. (I'm doing my best here. This would all sound so much better in an original.)

Af yge enneb inle mezre ygu . . . it feels 'like being inside wood' (as if I'd been spellbound, trapped, imprisoned within a tree, then axed). He's bruised all over his body, bruises brackish in colour like his skin's a passport cover, or as if his insides have been stamped with the splotch of poisonous berries——apparitions smeared across his stomach, faces null like navels. Everything hurts, his ribs hurt. His arms and legs feel shorter, he feels smaller, like a boy, younger than a boy. Wondering, wondering——what miracle decoction was that? what potion that stranger bruin conked me out with?

He's cold, wearing less clothes than he had been. Less a jacket, there's nothing returned to his pockets, there's no wallet, no return tix or pass. No oily key hard alongside his hardness, his wakingtime erection. An eye is swollen, a lip bleeds, he feels like he's broken a bone in his cheek. In his throat. He is thirsty——he goes.

The trickle is from a nearby stream whose water could not be anything but fresh, flowing, as even he's aware, from uphill even sweeter.

He follows, follows the stream's sharp dark carving of the hill, pausing only to wash himself and sip at a knotted pond, continuing.

This compulsion to ignore the fakeries and secondlives, for the origin, the source——he wants not the trickled down, he wants the wellspring only.

He trails through the woods, along the weedy banks in squeaking sneakers. The grain grades steeply, while the pits he has to avoid on his way are not wells to other worlds but the wet sucking prints of the outsize dogs that roam here. The big shaggy shepherding monstrosities he could ride atop——they prowl patrol around the summit's settlement, chaining the moat, the wall's circumsomnia.

Now he is hot, being so close to the sun——a lamp brought close by an invisible hand from above, swiftknuckled, silent. The summit rising only to flatten toward a desk, a desktop. And somewhere farfaraway——the sound of pages being turned or the clicking of keys——a chair unreclining, brought closer, closer.

Each of his bruises pulsates, pounds, giving off heat of its own, like he has circuits secreted inside, like overwork has ruined them.

The dogs he recognises, just then, he recognises as Sparkins——a litter of them, more, litters' clones of the one he'd had to be named after, nicknamed after, that one disastrous year before his parents were forced to sell it, or maybe, he'd suspected, put it down, because Dad in his couched craziness got allergic. But Sparkins a bit larger than the Sparkin he'd had, quite a bit larger, even from a distance. Enormous lumbering Sparkins trundling their guard, stepping over stumps, stepping through trunkhoarded piles of leafy cereal flakes, flecked with crystals of sugar, of salt. Blown piles up to the moat, then on the moat's other marge up to the fortress wall, blown spoons and bowls and the smothering plastic that bagged them——as if cumulus that'd been slammed by the wind into the trees and wall, becoming stilled, dispersed, disincarnated.

This city, being walled, is inherently attractive——not just in the artificial picturesque sense. When you are not wanted in, you want in, but maybe making you want in is the sense of a wall, its purpose. Where you are not needed you run to make yourself, you must, indispensable. He comes unheard and unseen, but perhaps the Sparkins are used to him already. Unheard because of their enlarged dogtags jingling in stride, jingling like bells. Unseen because he sneaks his way low and nimble. Toward the bridge's access, the bridge over the moat. The moat heaped with grey and creamcoloured boxes. With monitors and drives, modems and printers——all the elements of an obsolete technology, too useless to be recycled as another's access and so, their discard to hazard a fall: no water but a bog of coaxial cables in barbed coils, sharded screens of bridgelike wires, their innards exposed to spears and spikes, gutted lengths unwound to a murderous serration.

No foreigner storming invasion but a hero lost from a bedtime telling of immemorial nights, wandered from a page: he stands as if a pixel, a lone pix fixed at the draw-bridge's lip——a drawbridge, a moat, each flattened, flat, smooth the page, Reload.

To enter through the portcullis withdrawing, through its portal . . . (this is where I write from now——Dear Mom, cc: The End——I must have fainted).

I wake in a square, undressed but tended. My bruising beginning to subside. And in its stead, a glow fanning through me, as if the opening rose of health, as if vigour.

The town is a setting of lithic streets and alleys, the houses themselves logged of dilapidated wood——but lived in, not neglected, textured.

Nobody is around——no presences I sense directly——but I feel, I prickle as I feel——these floatings, these passings.

F

A brush of hair or a gusting sway, as if the skirt of the wind blowing by me, blushing up my cheeks. A skin's prick to horripilate the wrist, a nail's graze or a lovemark left by teeth. As I begin——this is how I begin——gradually, after days, a week, *to see*.

Everywhere——as if enclosed, as if my life's been flattened up against the seething surface of my eye——everywhere I look soon there are women, *there are girls*.

I see them, by seeing through them. Their beings projected onto every surface, on every ceiling and floor and sky, projecting across every window and alley's curve, across and as every doorway's gracious waist——the walls, visible through them in wrinkle crack and cellulite chip, in spall and score and peeling paint, temporarily aging them in their revenance. But then they float again, they pass again——eidola of posturing plank, with glints of screwy smiles——their youth preserved only in their motion.

Girls throughout alight and nude, or not nude but purified, thoroughly pristinated as I proceed——through the statics of climate——to recognise: Natashka one and another from that vid with the Cuban I think and yet another from a schoolyard seduction and still another from the bucked back of a moving truck and a girl I recall her name too, I think Masha, Sasha, Svetlana (trans. *luminance*)——and they are themselves but aren't, as they were both onscreen and you have to guess in life itself, but not.

You can speak to them but there's no indication, Mom, that they can hear you and certainly they can't speak to me, Mom, not yet——if they did then in what language?

You go to touch and you touch right through them. Snug a breast and end up feeling up a boulder, flick a lip and end rubbing tongue against a sill.

They just hover, Mom, amongst their daily tasks——gathering water they won't drink, steaming suppers they cannot eat, but I can.

I am sustained, they take good care, don't worry.

I've even stopped asking after Moc.

I'm sure, one day, I'll notice her appearance. As a shadow's missing features. As faced light thrown across a wall that is not home's.

Your message has been sent.

My message has been sent.

F

APPENDIX

MICHAEL AMHERST is a writer of fiction and non-fiction. His work has been published in the *Guardian*, the *Spectator* and *The White Review*, among others. He is also a Director of Just Detention International and campaigns against the abuse of those held in custody.

DAVID AUERBACH is a writer and software engineer living in New York. His work has appeared in the *Times Literary Supplement, n+1, Triple Canopy*, and the *Quarterly Conversation*. He is the author of http://waggish.org.

GIACONDA BELLI was born in Nicaragua. As well as novels, she has published six poetry collections. For poetry she has won the Casa de las Américas Prize, the Generación del 27 Prize, and the Ciudad de Melilla Prize. Her poems have been translated into German, Italian, French, English, Turkish, Portuguese and Russian.

JOSHUA COHEN is the author of the novels *Witz, A Heaven of Others*, and *Cadenza for the Schneidermann Violin Concerto*. A book of novellas, *Four New Messages*, will be published by Graywolf Press in August 2012, and an essay on the history of attention is forthcoming with *Notting Hill Editions* in 2013. Cohen is the New Books critic for *Harper's Magazine*. He lives in New York City.

EMILY CRITCHLEY holds a Ph.D in contemporary American women's poetry and philosophy from the University of Cambridge. She is the author of several critical articles – on poetry, philosophy and feminism – and several poetry chapbooks. *Her Selected Writing, Love / All That / & OK*, was published by Penned in the Margins in 2011. She teaches English and Creative Writing at the University of Greenwich, London.

SARAH HEGENBART is a curator, writer and researcher based in London. She curated Christoph Schlingensief's first solo exhibition in the UK, at the German Embassy in 2012. Sarah holds a Master's in Philosophy from the University of Oxford, and is currently researching the notion of beauty in contemporary arts for her doctorate.

CAMILLE HENROT's work has been exhibited at the Centre Pompidou, Musée d'Art Moderne de la Ville de Paris, the Palais de Tokyo, the Espace Paul Ricard, the Jeu de Paume, the Cartier Foundation, the Louis Vuitton Cultural Space, the Foundation Maeght, the collections of Saint-Cyprien, the Museum of Fine Arts of Bordeaux, Crac Alsace, and at Sungkok Art Museum in Seoul, the Palais des Beaux-Arts in Brussels, the Centre for Contemporary Images in Geneva, the Hara Museum in Tokyo and Oi Futuro Cultural Centre in Rio de Janeiro. Upcoming shows include 'Is it Possible to be a Revolutionary and Like Flowers?' at Kamel Mennour Gallery, New York and 'Jewels' at Rosascape, Paris.

FRANZISKA HOLSTEIN was born, and lives and works, in Leipzig. Her solo exhibitions include 'Kombi', Galerie Christian Ehrentraut, Berlin (2012); 'Franziska Holstein und Robert Seidel', Konrad–Adenauer–Stiftung, Berlin (2011); 'Brote/ Spiel', Galerie Christian Ehrentraut, Berlin (2009); 'PMFH', Galerie Spesshardt & Klein, 'Berlin PMFH / Meisterschuelerausstellung', Tapetenwerk, Leipzig (2008); 'Weekend', Marianne Boesky Gallery, New York (2007).

MAX MCGUINNESS teaches French at Columbia University in New York.

NIALL MCCLELLAND lives and works in Toronto. Recent solo exhibitions include 'One Turn Outta Turn' at Eleanor Harwood Gallery, San Francisco, and 'Highest Prices paid for Gold' at Clint Roenisch Gallery, Toronto. In June 2012 he was included in the group exhibtion 'Trans/FORM' at the Museum of Contemporary Canadian Art.

HERTA MÜLLER, born in Romania in 1953, worked as a translator and German teacher after completing her studies in German Literature. In 1987, she moved to Berlin and began to publish short stories, novels, and poetry collages. She won the Nobel Prize for Literature in 2009. Herta Müller's collages are available as art prints in a range of sizes and materials at www.DrNice.net

IVAN VLADISLAVIĆ is the author of the novels *THE RESTLESS SUPERMARKET, THE EXPLODED VIEW* and *DOUBLE NEGATIVE*. Among his other books are *PORTRAIT WITH KEYS*, an account of life in Johannesburg, and *THE LOSS LIBRARY*, a reflection on writing (and not writing). He sometimes works with visual artists and has edited volumes on architecture and art.

J. S. TENNANT works for PEN International and *THE WHITE REVIEW*. He has worked as a ghost writer, journalist and in publishing.

DAVID WINTERS is a literary and cultural critic. He has written for the *TIMES LITERARY SUPPLEMENT, BOOKFORUM*, the *LOS ANGELES REVIEW OF BOOKS* and others, and is a contributing editor at *3:AM MAGAZINE*.

THE WHITE REVIEW would like to thank the staff at Opera Village Africa for their assistance. To learn more about the project or to donate please visit: www.opendorf–afrika.com